Measuring Up®

to the
Georgia Performance Standards

and Success Strategies for the CRCT

Mathematics

This book is customized for Georgia and the lessons cover the Georgia Performance Standards for Mathematics. The Measuring Up® program includes instructional worktexts and Georgia Diagnostic Practice Tests, and Measuring Up® e-Path which are available separately.

Level
D

800-822-1080
www.PeoplesEducation.com

Peoples Education
Your partner in student success

Publisher: Diane Miller

Editorial Development: Inkwell Publishing Solutions, Inc./
Edutorial Services

Acting Editorial Director: Eugene McCormick

Supervising Editor: Lee Shenkman

Vice President of Marketing: Victoria Ameer Kiely

Director of Marketing: Melissa Dubno Geller

Vice President, Production and Manufacturing: Doreen Smith

Production Director: Nicole Dawson

Production: Argosy Publishing

Project Manager: Jennifer Tully

Photo Researcher/Permissions Manager: Kristine Liebman

Cover Designers: Chris Kennedy, Cynthia Mackowicz, Michele Sakow

Illustrators: Armando Báez, Salvatore Esposito, Rieko Radomski, Dan
Lish, Sharon MacGregor

Georgia Advisory Panel, Elementary School:

Jill Adams, Math Specialist, Columbia Elementary School,
DeKalb County Schools, GA

Mrs. Judith Berlage, Educator, Cobb County, GA

Kim C. Davis, EdS, Math Literacy Coach & PDS Director,
Gainesville City Schools

Teena Hardwick Curriculum Department, Cherokee County School District

Peoples Education™

Your partner in student success™

Copyright © 2007
Peoples Education, Inc.
299 Market Street
Saddle Brook, New Jersey 07663

ISBN 978-1-4138-4892-2
ISBN 1-4138-4892-3

Printed in the United States of America.

10   9   8   7   6   5   4   3   2   1

Measuring Up® Contents

CHAPTER 1 Place Value, Rounding, Addition, and Subtraction

CHAPTER 2 Multiplication

CHAPTER 3 Division

CHAPTER 4 Fractions

CHAPTER 5   Decimals

CHAPTER 6   Create and Extend Patterns

CHAPTER 7   Measurement

CHAPTER 8　Geometry

CHAPTER 9　Data Analysis

It's time for a full review of the Georgia Mathematics Performance Standards. This review includes challenging, higher-level thinking questions that will help you prepare for mastery of mathematics.

Student Resources
Provided are definitions and explanations of mathematics terminology.

Lesson Correlation to the Georgia Mathematics Grade 4 Performance Standards

This worksheet is customized to the Georgia Mathematics Performance Standards
and will help you prepare for mastery of Mathematics.

Georgia Performance Standards—Mathematics	Lessons
M4A. Algebra **Students will investigate and represent mathematical relationships between quantities using mathematical expressions in problem-solving situations.**	
M4A1. Students will represent and interpret mathematical relationships in quantitative expressions.	
a. Understand and apply patterns and rules to describe relationships and solve problems.	38, 39, 40, 41, Ch. 6 AC
b. Represent unknowns using symbols, such as ? and .	42, 43, Ch. 6 AC
c. Write and evaluate mathematical expressions using symbols and different values.	42, 43, Ch. 6 AC
M4D. Data Analysis **Students will gather, organize, and display data. They will also compare features of graphs.**	
M4D1. Students will gather, organize, and display data according to the situation and compare related features.	
a. Represent data in bar, line and pictographs.	57, 58, 59, Ch. 9 AC
b. Investigate the features and tendencies of graphs.	57, 58, 59, Ch. 9 AC
c. Compare different graphical representations for a given set of data.	61, Ch. 9 AC
d. Identify missing information and duplications in data.	60, Ch. 9 AC
M4G. Geometry **Students will understand and construct plane and solid geometric figures. They will also graph points on the coordinate plane.**	
M4G1. Students will define and identify the characteristics of geometric figures through examination and construction.	47, Ch. 7 AC
a. Examine and compare angles in order to classify and identify triangles by their angles.	51, Ch. 8 AC
b. Describe parallel and perpendicular lines in plane geometric figures.	49, Ch. 8 AC
c. Examine and classify quadrilaterals (including parallelograms, squares, rectangles, trapezoids, and rhombi).	52, 54, Ch. 8 AC
d. Compare and contrast the relationships among quadrilaterals.	52, 56, Ch. 8 AC
M4G2. Students will understand fundamental solid figures.	
a. Compare and contrast a cube and a rectangular prism in terms of the number and shape of their faces, edges, and vertices.	53, Ch. 8 AC
b. Describe parallel and perpendicular lines and planes in connection with the rectangular prism.	53, Ch. 8 AC
c. Construct/collect models for solid geometric figures (cube, prisms, cylinder, etc.).	53, Ch. 8 AC

continued

AC = Applying Concepts

Georgia Performance Standards—Mathematics	Lessons
M4G3. Students will use the coordinate system.	
a. Understand and apply ordered pairs in the first quadrant of the coordinate system.	55, Ch. 8 AC
b. Locate a point in the first quadrant in the coordinate plane and name the ordered pair.	55, Ch. 8 AC
c. Graph ordered pairs in the first quadrant.	55, Ch. 8 AC
M4M. Measurement **Students will measure weight in appropriate metric and standard units.** **They will also measure angles.**	
M4M1. Students will understand the concept of weight and how to measure it.	
a. Use standard and metric units to measure the weight of objects.	45, 46, Ch. 7 AC
b. Know units used to measure weight (gram, kilogram, ounces, pounds and tons).	45, 46, Ch. 7 AC
c. Compare one unit to another within a single system of measurement.	44, 45, 46, Ch. 7 AC
M4M2. Students will understand the concept of *angles* and how to measure *it*.	
a. Use tools, such as a protractor or angle ruler, and other methods such as paper folding, drawing a diagonal in a square, to measure angles.	50, Ch. 8 AC
b. Understand the meaning and measure of a half rotation (180°) and a full rotation (360°).	54, Ch. 8 AC
M4N. Number and Operations **Students will further develop their understanding of whole numbers and master the four basic operations with whole numbers by solving problems. They will also understand rotunding and when to appropriately use it. Students will add and subtract decimal fractions and common fractions with common denominators.**	
M4N1. Students will further develop their understanding of how whole numbers are represented in the base-ten numeration system.	
a. Identify place value names and places from hundredths through one million.	1, 2, 3, 6, Ch. 1 AC, 30, Ch. 5 AC
b. Equate a number's word name, its standard form, and its expanded form.	1, 2, Ch. 1 AC
M4N2. Students will understand and apply the concept of rounding numbers.	
a. Round numbers to the nearest ten, hundred, or thousand.	4, Ch. 1 AC
b. Describe situations in which rounding numbers would be appropriate and determine whether to round to the nearest ten, hundred, or thousand.	3, 4, 7, Ch. 1 AC
c. Understand the meaning of rounding a decimal fraction to the nearest whole number.	32, Ch. 5 AC
d. Represent the results of computation as a rounded number when appropriate and estimate a sum or difference by rounding numbers.	7, Ch. 1 AC

continued

AC = Applying Concepts

Georgia Performance Standards—Mathematics	Lessons
M4N3. Students will solve problems involving multiplication of 2-3 digit numbers by 1-2 digit numbers.	9, 10, 12, 13, 15, Ch. 2 AC
M4N4. Students will further develop their understanding of division of whole numbers and divide in problem solving situations without calculators.	
a. Know the division facts with understanding and fluency.	16, 17, 19, 20, Ch. 3 AC
b. Solve problems involving division by a 2-digit number (including those that generate a remainder).	19, Ch. 3 AC
c. Understand the relationship between dividend, divisor, quotient, and remainder.	17, 18, 20, Ch. 3 AC
d. Understand and explain the effect on the quotient of multiplying or dividing both the divisor and dividend by the same number. (2050 ÷ 50 yields the same answer as 205 ÷ 5).	20, 21, Ch. 3 AC
M4N5. Students will further develop their understanding of the meaning of decimal fractions and use them in computations.	
a. Understand decimal fractions are a part of the base-ten system.	30, 37, Ch. 5 AC
b. Understand the relative size of numbers and order two digit decimal fractions.	31, Ch. 5 AC
c. Add and subtract both one and two digit decimal fractions.	33, 34, Ch. 5 AC
d. Model multiplication and division of decimal fractions by whole numbers.	35, 36, Ch. 5 AC
e. Multiply and divide both one and two digit decimal fractions by whole numbers.	35, 36, Ch. 5 AC
M4N6. Students will further develop their understanding of the meaning of common fractions and use them in computations.	23
a. Understand representations of simple equivalent fractions.	24, Ch. 4 AC
b. Add and subtract fractions and mixed numbers with common denominators. (Denominators should not exceed twelve.)	25, 26, 27, 28, 29, Ch. 4 AC
c. Convert and use mixed numbers and improper fractions interchangeably.	23, 27, 28, Ch. 4 AC
M4N7. Students will explain and use properties of the four arithmetic operations to solve and check problems.	
a. Describe situations in which the four operations may be used and the relationships among them.	22, Ch. 3 AC, 40, 48, Ch. 7 AC
b. Compute using the order of operations, including parentheses.	5, Ch. 1 AC, 22, Ch. 3 AC
c. Compute using the commutative, associative, and distributive properties.	11, Ch. 2 AC, 22, Ch. 3 AC
d. Use mental math and estimation strategies to compute.	5, 7, Ch. 1 AC, 14, Ch. 2 AC, 17, 21, Ch. 3 AC

continued

AC = Applying Concepts

Georgia Performance Standards—Mathematics	Lessons
M4P. Process Skills Students will apply mathematical concepts and skills in the context of authentic problems and will understand concepts rather than merely following a sequence of procedures. Students will use the process standards as a way of acquiring and using content knowledge.	
M4P1. Using the appropriate technology, students will solve problems that arise in mathematics and in other contexts.	
a. Solve non-routine word problems using the strategies of work backwards, use or make a table, and make an organized list as well as all strategies learned in previous grades.	14, 15, Ch. 2 AC, Ch. 4 AC, 43, Ch. 6 AC
b. Solve single and multi-step routine word problems related to all appropriate fourth grade math standards.	6, Ch. 1 AC, 16, 17, 18, 19, 21, 22, Ch. 3 AC, 23, 24, 25, 26, 29, Ch. 4 AC, 32, 33, 34, 37, Ch. 5 AC, 40, 42, Ch. 6 AC, 44, Ch. 7 AC, 62, Ch. 9 AC
c. Determine the operation(s) needed to solve a problem.	5, 8, Ch. 1 AC, Ch. 2 AC, 21, 22, Ch. 3 AC, 38, 39, 40, 41, Ch. 6 AC
d. Determine the most efficient way to solve a problem (mentally, paper/pencil, or calculator).	4, 7, 8, Ch. 1 AC, 11, Ch. 2 AC, 32
M4P2. Students will investigate, develop, and evaluate mathematical arguments.	10, Ch. 2 AC, 18, Ch. 3 AC, 45, Ch. 7 AC, 56
M4P3. Students will use the language of mathematics to express ideas precisely.	1, 2, 6, Ch. 1 AC, 9, Ch. 2 AC, 31, 33, 34, Ch. 5 AC, 49, 51, 52, 55, 56, Ch. 8 AC
M4P4. Students will understand how mathematical ideas interconnect and build on one another and apply mathematics in other content areas.	1, 2, 4, Ch. 1 AC, 13, Ch. 2 AC, 16, 19, Ch. 3 AC, 30, Ch. 5 AC, Ch. 8 AC, 61
M4P5. Students will create and use pictures, manipulatives, models, and symbols to organize, record, and communicate mathematical ideas.	3, Ch. 1 AC, 9, 12, 13, Ch. 2 AC, 23, 24, 25, 26, 27, 28, 29, Ch. 4 AC, 30, 31, 35, 36, 37, Ch. 5 AC, 38, Ch. 6 AC, 47, 48, Ch. 7 AC, 49, 50, 51, 52, 53, 54, Ch. 8 AC, 57, 58, 60, Ch. 9 AC

AC = Applying Concepts

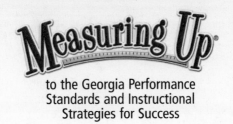

to the Georgia Performance Standards and Instructional Strategies for Success

Dear Student,

How do you get better at anything you do? You practice! Just like with sports or other activities, the way to success in school is practice, practice, practice.

This book will help you review and practice mathematics strategies and skills. These are the strategies and skills you need to know to measure up to the Georgia Performance Standards (GPS) for your grade. Practicing these skills and strategies now will help you do better in your work all year.

This book has nine chapters that review place-value concepts; computing and estimating with whole numbers; fractions; decimals; algebra concepts; measurement; geometry; and data-analysis.

Each lesson has four main sections:

- **Focus on GPS** introduces the skills covered in the lesson. Important vocabulary is introduced to help you communicate your understanding of mathematics concepts.

- **Guided Instruction** shows you the steps and skills necessary to solve problems.

- **Apply the GPS** helps you practice important concepts and skills reviewed in the lesson.

- **CRCT Practice** gives you experience in responding to questions in test format.

This book gives you lots of chances to practice multiple-choice questions like the ones you will see on tests this year. The **Applying Concepts** review sections at the end of each chapter and at the end of the book include more difficult multiple-choice questions that will help sharpen your higher-level thinking skills.

Have a great year!

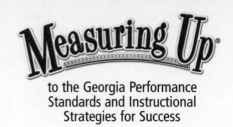

Measuring Up®

to the Georgia Performance
Standards and Instructional
Strategies for Success

To Parents and Families,

All students need mathematics skills to succeed. Georgia educators have created grade-appropriate standards called the Georgia Performance Standards, or GPS, for Mathematics. The GPS describe what all Georgia students should know at each grade level.

Measuring Up® is 100% customized to the GPS for mathematics for grade 4. These standards emphasize higher-level thinking skills. Students must learn to analyze, interpret, and generalize, as well as recall facts and operate with numbers. This book will help your child review the skills and concepts described in the standards and prepare for grade 4 mathematics tests. It contains:

- **Lessons** that focus on practicing the skills described in the Georgia Performance Standards;

- **Guided Instruction,** in which students are shown the steps and skills necessary to solve a variety of mathematical problems;

- **Apply the Georgia Performance Standards,** which provides practice with concepts and skills reviewed in the lesson;

- **CRCT Practice,** which shows how individual standards can be understood through answering multiple-choice questions;

- **Applying Concepts,** which gives practice with multiple-choice questions that require higher-level thinking skills.

For success in school and in the real world, your child needs to be successful in mathematics. Get involved! Your involvement is crucial to your child's success. Here are some suggestions:

- Keep mathematics alive in your home. Involve your child in activities that use mathematics, such as mixing recipes, counting coins, telling time, and identifying geometric shapes and patterns.

- Look for ways mathematics is used when you are out with your family. Encourage your child to count your change after making a purchase, read the items and prices in a restaurant menu, identify shapes such as spheres and cubes in real objects, and add or subtract to find how many there are or how many are left in real-life situations.

- Ask your child to talk and write about what they have learned in mathematics. Always encourage them to use mathematical language.

- Encourage your child to take the time to review and check his or her homework. Finding a solution is just one part of solving a problem. Ask your child to tell why his or her answers are reasonable and make sense.

Work with us this year to ensure your child's success. Mathematics is essential not only for success in school but in the world as well.

Peoples education™
Your partner in student success™

What's Ahead in Measuring Up®

This book was created for Georgia students like you. Each lesson, question, and problem will help you master the Georgia Performance Standards for Mathematics and prepare for any rigorous assignments you are required to take in Mathematics this year and in the future. It will also help you do well on other mathematics tests you take during the school year.

About the Georgia Performance Standards

Georgia educators have developed standards for mathematics. They are called the Georgia Performance Standards, or GPS. They spell out what all students at each grade level should know.

Measuring Up® on Multiple-Choice Questions

A multiple-choice question has two parts. The first part is the stem, or question. It has a number in front of it. The second part is made up of the answer choices. Each answer choice has a letter A, B, C, or D in front of it. You will be asked to read each question and then circle the letter for the best answer.

Some of the multiple-choice questions have a graph or table. You will need to read information from the graph or table to solve the problem.

For example, in the question below, you will need to read the information in the table, select the answer choice that seems most reasonable, then circle the letter next to that answer.

1. The table below shows the cost of flowers in a flower shop.

Number of Flowers	Cost
4	$1.00
5	$1.25
6	$1.50
7	$1.75

How much does one flower cost?

A. 10 cents

B. 20 cents

C. 25 cents

D. 50 cents

By studying the pattern in the table, you can see that each flower costs 25 cents. So C is the correct answer. Notice how to mark your answer.

Here are some strategies for answering multiple-choice questions:

- Try to work the problem without looking at the answer choices. Once you have solved the problem, compare your answer with the answer choices.

- Eliminate answer choices you know are wrong. Then choose from the answers that are left.

- Some questions will be more difficult than others. The problem may require an extra step, or you may need to look for which answers do not apply.

- Even if you don't know the answer, you can make a good guess based on what you know and get the right answer.

- Check and double-check your answers before you turn in the test. Be sure of your answers.

Higher-Level Thinking Skills

Higher-level thinking skills are important. When you use higher-level thinking skills, you do more than just recall information. Some questions ask you to find and continue a pattern, understand and use information in a table or graph, or use a number line. Instead of adding or subtracting to solve a problem, you may need to use more than one operation to solve a real-world problem. In Measuring Up® , the higher-level thinking skills questions are starred.

Measuring Up® with Applying Concepts

A special feature of Measuring Up® is **Applying Concepts**. It was created to give you practice and build your confidence for taking hard tests. The more you practice answering difficult questions, the more prepared you will be to succeed. At the end of each chapter, an **Applying Concepts** section reviews the chapter concepts and skills. At the end of the book, there is a longer **Applying Concepts** that reviews Georgia Performance Standards covered throughout the book.

Tips for Measuring Up®

There are some general strategies you can use to succeed. Here are a few useful tips:

- Start getting ready now. Spend a few minutes each day practicing answers to test questions. If you work hard, you will probably do well.

- Get a good night's sleep.

- Eat a good breakfast.

- Remember the story of the little engine that kept saying , "I think I can. I think I can." Keep telling yourself that you will do well. That's what it means to "think positively."

You will learn a lot in Measuring Up® You will review and practice the Georgia Performance Standards. You will practice for assessments you will take this year. Finally, you will build your stamina to answer tough questions. You will more than measure up. You'll be a smashing success!

M4N1.a	Identify place value names and places from hundredths through one million.
M4N1.b	Equate a number's word name, its standard form, and its expanded form.
M4P3	Students will use the language of mathematics to express ideas precisely.
M4P4	Students will understand how mathematical ideas interconnect and build on one another and apply mathematics in other content areas.

You can use place value to help you find a number's word name and value. A place value chart shows the value of each digit in a number. Each period or group of three digits in a number is separated with a comma. You can also use expanded form to show the value of the digits in a number, as shown below:

$$7,965 \longrightarrow 7,000 + 900 + 60 + 5$$

Guided Instruction

Problem

The height of Mount Olympus in Washington is 7,965 feet. What is the name for the number 7,965?

Step 1 Write the number in the place-value chart. Include a comma between the thousands period and the ones period.

hundred thousands	ten thousands	one thousands	hundreds	tens	ones
		7,	9	6	5

What is the place of the digit 7 in 7,965? What is its value?

_____

Step 2 Find the word name of the number.

Write the number of thousands. Then write the number of ones.

__7__ thousand, __9__ __6__ __5__

Change the number to words.

seven thousand, nine hundred _____

Solution

What is the word name for the number 7,965?

_____

Apply the GPS

Write the word name for each number in the table.

Name of Island	Area (in square miles)
Caviana	1,918
King William	5,062
Sardinia	9,301

1. Caviana _____

2. King William _____

3. Sardinia _____

Write the place of the underlined digit in each number.

4. 3,267 _____   **5.** 4,019 _____

Write the value of the underlined digit in each number.

6. 2,734 _____   **7.** 5,860 _____

Write each number in expanded form.

8. 3,785 _____

9. 6,014 _____

Write the standard form of each number.

10. 7,000 + 500 + 90 + 3 _____   **11.** 9,000 + 200 + 1 _____

Write your answer to each question.

12. How many digits are in the number "seventeen thousand, nine hundred forty"?

_____

13. In which of the two numbers below does the digit 7 have a value of 7? Explain.

     712   5,397

_____

_____

_____

CRCT Practice

Directions: Choose the best answer for each question. Circle the letter for the answer you have chosen.

1. What is the place value for the underlined digit in 5,749?

    A. hundreds

    B. ones

    C. ten thousands

    D. thousands

Use the table below to answer questions 2 and 3.

Height of Waterfalls

Waterfall Name	Height (in feet)
Glass	1,325
Tugela	2,014

2. What is the expanded form of the height of the Tugela waterfalls?

    A. 1,000 + 3 + 2 + 5

    B. 1,000 + 300 + 20 + 5

    C. 2,000 + 1 + 4

    D. 2,000 + 10 + 4

3. Look at the heights of the two waterfalls. Which statement is NOT true?

    A. There is a 3 in the hundred place of one number.

    B. There is 5 in the ones place of one number.

    C. There is one 2 in the ones place of one number and another 2 in the thousands place of the second number.

    D. There is one 1 in the thousands place of one number and another 1 in the tens place of the second number.

4. Which name is the same as the number 8,306?

    A. eight thousand, thirty-six

    B. eight thousand, three hundred six

    C. eighty thousand, three hundred six

    D. eighty-three thousand, six

 5. The table below shows the results of the town election for mayor.

Name	Number of Votes
Bradley	6,438
Diaz	9,276
Jensen	1,604
Marino	4,865

Which number of votes has the digit 6 with a value of 600?

    A. 1,604

    B. 4,865

    C. 6,438

    D. 9,276

Lesson 2 Place Value to One Million

M4N1.a	Identify place value names and places from hundredths through one million.
M4N1.b	Equate a number's word name, its standard form, and its expanded form.
M4P3	Students will use the language of mathematics to express ideas precisely.
M4P4	Students will understand how mathematical ideas interconnect and build on one another and apply mathematics in other content areas.

You can use place value to help you find a number's value and word name.

Guided Instruction

Problem

In the year 2000, the number of people in Clayton County in the state of Georgia was 236,517. What are the values of the digits in the number 236,517?

You can use a place-value chart to find the value of each digit in a number.

Step 1 Write the number in the place-value chart.

MILLIONS			THOUSANDS			ONES		
hundred millions	ten millions	one millions	hundred thousands	ten thousands	one thousands	hundreds	tens	ones
			2	3	6	5	1	7

Write the word name of the number.

two hundred thirty-six thousand, five hundred seventeen

Look at the chart. What digit is in the ten thousands place? What is the value of the digit? _____

Step 2 Write the value of each digit of the number. Start from the left. Add each value to complete the expanded form of the number.

200,000 + 30,000 + 6,000 + 500 + 10 + 7

Solution

What are the values of the digits in the number 236,517?

_____

Apply the GPS   **Write the word name for the population of each county.**

1.   Lancaster County: 470,658

_____

2.   Prince George's County: 801,515

_____

Write the value of the underlined digit in each number.

3.   246,758 _____   **4.**   936,014 _____

Write the place of the underlined digit in each number.

5.   329,481 _____   **6.**   657,091 _____

Write each number in expanded form.

7.   502,481 _____

8.   613,097 _____

Write the standard form of each number.

9.   600,000 + 90,000 + 7,000 + 30 + 8 _____

10. 800,000 + 5,000 + 700 + 20 + 4 _____

Write your answer to each question.

11. Write a number that has a 3 in the hundred thousands place.

_____

Write the value of the 3 in the hundred thousands place. _____

12. A company sold 999,999 cars. Then it sold one more car. Write the new number

of cars sold. _____

What is the greatest place value of the new number? _____

CRCT Practice

Directions: Choose the best answer for each question. Circle the letter for the answer you have chosen.

1. Which is four hundred eighty-two thousand, six hundred ninety-five?

   A. 400,820,695

   B. 482,600,95

   C. 4,826,195

   D. 482,695

2. The table below shows two numbers that Anna and Jerry wrote in expanded form.

Name	Number in Expanded Form
Anna	600,000 + 3,000 + 50 + 7
Jerry	400,000 + 20,000 + 10 + 8

   What is the standard form of Jerry's number?

   A. 402,108

   B. 420,018

   C. 600,357

   D. 630,057

3. What is the value of the underlined digit in 43,816?

   A. 30,000

   B. 13,000

   C. 3,000

   D. 3

4. Which crayon represents the hundred thousands place?

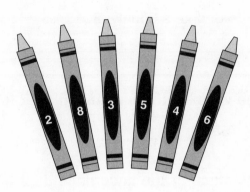

   A. 2

   B. 3

   C. 5

   D. 6

5. What is the expanded form of 803,504?

   A. 800,000 + 30,000 + 50 + 4

   B. 800,000 + 3,000 + 500 + 4

   C. 800,000 + 3,000 + 50 + 40

   D. 800,000 + 3,000 + 50 + 4

     Measuring Up® to the Georgia Performance Standards

Lesson 3 Compare and Order Numbers

M4N1.a	Identify place value names and places from hundredths through one million.
M4N2.b	Describe situations in which rounding numbers would be appropriate and determine whether to round to the nearest ten, hundred, or thousand.
M4P5	Students will create and use pictures, manipulatives, models, and symbols to organize, record, and communicate mathematical ideas.

You can use place value to compare and order whole numbers. Compare or relate numbers to see if one is greater than (>), less than (<), or equal to (=) another. The symbols < and > point to the smaller number.

Guided Instruction

Problem

> The area of Spring Mountains Park is 312,683 acres. The area of Grand Teton Park is 310,027 acres. Which park has a greater number of acres?

Use a place-value chart to compare the digits in both numbers. Work from left to right.

Step 1 Write both numbers in the place-value chart.

millions	hundred thousands	ten thousands	thousands	hundreds	tens	ones
	3	1	2	6	8	3
	3	1	0	0	2	7

Step 2 Which is the greatest place value where the digits are different?

_____

Step 3 Compare the digits in the first place where they are different.

Use > or <: 2 ◯ 0

Step 4 Now write >, <, or = to compare the numbers.

31**2**,683 ◯ 31**0**,027

Solution

> Which park has a greater number of acres?
>
> _____

Another Example

A number line can also help you compare and order numbers.

On a number line, the numbers increase from left to right.

Apply the GPS

Compare. Write >, <, or = for each.

1. 14,725 ◯ 9,638

2. 7,843 ◯ 7,850

3. 539,241 ◯ 570,120

4. 946,028 ◯ 946,028

Which number is the greatest in each group? Write the number.

5. 356,129   359,600   207,261   332,784   _____

6. 6,294   6,902   6,958   6,327   _____

Which number is the least in each group? Write the number.

7. 112,418   97,320   96,512   102,684   _____

8. 8,415   8,902   8,679   8,463   _____

Write the order of the numbers in each group from least to greatest.

9. 475,903   478,285   469,863   _____, _____, _____

10. 9,924   9,087   9,975   _____, _____, _____

Write the order of the numbers in each group from greatest to least.

11. 629,998   1,000,000   634,100   _____, _____, _____

12. 12,370   9,258   13,001   _____, _____, _____

Use the table for questions 13–14.

13. Which two parks have a much greater area than the other two parks?

_____

14. Explain how you arrived at your answer to question 13.

_____

_____

Area of National Parks

Name of Park	Area (in acres)
Capitol Reef	241,904
Kings Canyon	461,901
Mount Rainier	235,613
Sequoia	402,482

CRCT Practice Directions: Choose the best answer for each question.
Circle the letter for the answer you have chosen.

1. Which number is the greatest?

   A. 672,015

   B. 671,983

   C. 684,204

   D. 639,578

2. The table below shows the number of acres in each park.

Name of Park	Number of Acres
Mono Basin	115,600
Mount Rogers	114,520
Mount St. Helens	112,593

Which group shows the number of acres ordered from least to greatest?

   A. 115,600, 114,520, 112,593

   B. 114,520, 112,593, 115,600

   C. 112,593, 115,600, 114,520

   D. 112,593, 114,520, 115,600

 3. Nancy changed the 4 in the number 384,251 to a 7. How did she change the value?

   A. increased by 3,000

   B. increased by 300

   C. decreased by 3,000

   D. decreased by 300

 4. Use the table below.

Treetop Park Visitors	
Day of Week	**Estimated Number of Visitors**
Thursdays	170,000
Fridays	?
Saturdays	250,000

Treetop Park gets about ten thousand fewer visitors on Fridays than on Saturdays. Which is about the number of visitors the park gets on Fridays?

   A. 150,000

   B. 240,000

   C. 260,000

   D. 350,000

Lesson 4 Round Whole Numbers

M4N2.a	Round numbers to the nearest ten, hundred, or thousand.
M4N2.b	Describe situations in which rounding numbers would be appropriate and determine whether to round to the nearest ten, hundred, or thousand.
M4P1.d	Students will understand how mathematical ideas interconnect and build on one another and apply mathematics in other content areas.
M4P4	Determine the most efficient way to solve a problem (mentally, paper/pencil, or calculator).

You can use place value to round numbers to the nearest ten, nearest hundred, or nearest thousand. To **round** a number means to bring it up or down to the nearest ten, hundred, and so on. Use rounded numbers to find an **estimate**, or a number close to an exact number.

Guided Instruction

Problem

Pine School has 7,258 books in its library. What is the number 7,258 rounded to the nearest ten, to the nearest hundred, and to the nearest thousand?

You can use number lines or digits to round whole numbers.

Step 1 Draw a number line. If you are rounding to the nearest **ten**, show the greater ten and the lesser ten for the number.

7,250   7,260

7,258

Step 2 Look at the number line. Find which ten the number is nearer to.

7,258 rounded to the nearest ten is _____.

Step 3 You can also look at the digits of the number. Underline the digit in the place you want to round to. To round to the nearest **hundred**, underline the digit in the _____ place.

7,258

Step 4 Circle the digit to the right of the underlined place. If the circled digit is 5 or greater, round up to the greater hundred. If it is less than 5, round down to the lesser hundred.

7,258

Since 5 = 5, round up.

7,258 rounded to the nearest hundred is _____.

Choose a method to round 7,258 to the nearest **thousand**.

Solution

What is the number 7,258 rounded to each place?
nearest ten? _____, nearest hundred? _____ nearest thousand? _____.

Apply the GPS   **Round each number to the nearest ten.**

1. 3,647 _____

2. 512 _____

3. 90,725 _____

Round each number to the nearest hundred.

4. 65,857 _____

5. 248,639 _____

6. 7,094 _____

Round each number to the nearest thousand.

7. 1,296 _____

8. 503,421 _____

9. 99,635 _____

Mark each number on the number line below. Then round each number to the nearest hundred.

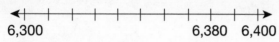

6,300   6,380   6,400

10. 6,320 _____

11. 6,350 _____

Solve each problem.

12. Elm School has 5,273 books in its library. What is the number 5,273 rounded to the nearest ten? _____

13. Mr. Sims is selling some fruit from a box. He has 991 fruits left in the box. What is the number 991 rounded to the nearest hundred? _____

14. Tina estimated that 3,500 people came to see the school play. She rounded to the nearest hundred to get her estimate. Name one number that Tina could have started with. Explain why 3,500 is the nearest hundred for your number.

_____

_____

_____

CRCT Practice **Directions: Choose the best answer for each question. Circle the letter for the answer you have chosen.**

1. Round **7,802** to the nearest ten.

   A. 7,800

   B. 7,810

   C. 7,900

   D. 8,802

2. What is the missing number at the arrow?

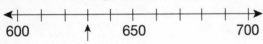

   A. 649

   B. 648

   C. 630

   D. 620

3. A school bus holds 100 students. About how many buses will the school need for 395 students?

   A. 3

   B. 4

   C. 40

   D. 400

Use the table below to answer questions 4–5.

Students in Public Schools

State	Number of Students
Arkansas	450,985
Kansas	470,957
Nevada	369,498
Utah	489,072

4. Which is the number of students in Kansas schools rounded to the nearest thousand?

   A. 500,000

   B. 471,000

   C. 470,000

   D. 451,000

5. Which is NOT a rounded number of students for Utah?

   A. 500,000

   B. 490,000

   C. 489,000

   D. 488,000

Lesson 5 Use Mental Math to Add or Subtract

M4N7.b	Compute using the commutative, associative, and distributive properties.
M4N7.d	Use mental math and estimation strategies to compute.
M4P1.c	Determine the operation(s) needed to solve a problem.

You can use place value and properties to add and subtract mentally. Sometimes you can add or subtract just in one place instead of with every digit in a number.

Guided Instruction

Problem
Ivy School had 8,394 students. Then 20 students moved away. What is the new number of students at Ivy School?

You can work with digits in a place to add or subtract in your head.

Step 1 Find the place of the digits that you will be adding or subtracting.

Since you need to subtract 20, subtract in the tens place.

The digit in the tens place in 8,394 is _____.

Step 2 Use mental math to add or subtract.

Think: 8,39**4** $\longrightarrow$ 9 tens
$-$ **2**0 $\longrightarrow$ $-$ 2 tens
                                 7 tens

The digit now in the tens place for the new number is _____.

Solution What is the new number of students at Ivy School? _____.

Other Examples

Sometimes addition properties can help you order numbers for mental math.

Addition Property	Mental Math Example
Commutative Property Changing the order of the numbers added does not change the sum. $5 + 16 = 16 + 5$	Al saw 13 cats and 186 dogs. What is the total? You can do this: Instead of this: 186 13 $+\ 13$ $+\ 186$
Associative Property The way numbers are grouped to add does not change the sum. $(2 + 3) + 8 = 2 + (3 + 8)$	Sue read 192, then 37, then 8 pages of a book. How many pages has she read in all? You can do this: Instead of this: $(192 + 8) + 37$ $(192 + 37) + 8$

Apply the GPS   Use mental math. Subtract 10 from each number. What digit is now in the tens place?

1. 9,364 _____

2. 72,908 _____

3. 865,217 _____

Use mental math. Add 4 thousands to each number. What is the new number?

4. 23,596 _____

5. 315,042 _____

6. 6,403 _____

Write the order in which you would add the numbers. Find each sum.

7. Joe read 211 pages of a book. Then he read 56 pages and 9 pages of the book. How many pages has he read in all?

(_____ + _____) + _____ = _____

8. Lora has 21 large buttons. She has 758 small buttons. What is the total number of buttons Lora has?

(_____ + _____) = _____

Use mental math to find each sum or difference.

9.
    4,879
−   60

10.
    13
+ 576

11.
    99,580
−   5,400

Solve each problem. Explain your mental math method for solving the problem.

12. Flagtop Park had 89,768 seats. The park took away 600 of the seats. What digit is in the hundreds place for the new number of seats? _____

_____

13. At Pineland Park, school children planted 100 trees this month and 200 trees last month. Before that, they had planted 5,426 trees over ten years. What was the new total number of trees planted? _____

_____

14. Ms. Reed thinks she will drive her car for 5,000 miles this year. She has driven her car for 23,145 miles so far. What would the new number of miles in all be?

_____

_____

CRCT Practice

Directions: Choose the best answer for each question. Circle the letter for the answer you have chosen.

1. Subtract 10 from 8,903. What digit is now in the tens place?

    A   0

    B. 1

    C. 8

    D. 9

2. The table below shows the number of books sold by two top bookstores.

Name	Number of Books
Store A	270,403
Store B	253,689

If Store B sells one thousand of its books, what digit will be in the thousands place for Store B's new number of books?

    A. 1

    B. 2

    C. 4

    D. 9

3. At Grove School, 17 new children arrived this month. Last month, 3 new children arrived. Before that, the school had 254 children. Which shows how to find the new total number of children at Grove School?

    A. $254 + 3 - 17$

    B. $254 - 17 - 3$

    C. $(17 + 3) + 254$

    D. $(17 + 254) - 3$

4. The table below shows the number of seats at three city ball fields.

Field Name	Number of Seats
Ace Arena	27,973
Champion	25,450
River View	38,061

Champion Field will put in 3,000 new seats. What will the new number of seats at Champion Field be?

    A. 28,750

    B. 28,450

    C. 25,750

    D. 22,450

Focus on GPS

Lesson 6 **Addition and Subtraction Problems**

M4N1.a	Identify place value numbers and places from hundredths through one million.
M4P1.b	Solve single and multi-step routine word problems related to all appropriate fourth grade math standards.
M4P3	Students will use the language of mathematics to express ideas precisely.

When you add and subtract, sometimes you need to regroup.

To **regroup** means to rename a number.

When you add, regroup 10 ones as 1 ten, and 10 tens as 1 hundred, and 10 hundreds as 1 thousand.

When you subtract, regroup 1 ten as 10 ones, and 1 hundred as 10 tens, and 1 thousand as 10 hundreds.

Guided Instruction

Problem 1	Voters in Eton chose to build a park either at Li Road or Elm Way. 376 voters chose Li Road. 258 voters chose Elm Way. How many voters voted in all?

You can add to find the total number of voters.

Step 1   Write the addition in columns. Line up the digits.

First, add the ones.

_____ ones + _____ ones = _____ ones.

Are there 10 or more ones? _____

Do you need to regroup? _____

Regroup 14 ones as _____ ten and _____ ones.

$$\begin{array}{r} 3\,7\,\mathbf{6} \\ +\,2\,5\,\mathbf{8} \\ \hline \end{array}$$

Step 2   Add the tens.

_____ ten + _____ tens + _____ tens = _____ tens.

Are there 10 or more tens? _____

Do you need to regroup? _____

Regroup 13 tens as _____ hundred and _____ tens.

$$\begin{array}{r} {\scriptstyle 1} \\ 3\,\mathbf{7}\,6 \\ +\,2\,\mathbf{5}\,8 \\ \hline 4 \end{array}$$

Step 3   Add the hundreds.

Why is it important to always line up the digits?

_____

_____

$$\begin{array}{r} {\scriptstyle 1} \\ \mathbf{3}\,7\,6 \\ +\,\mathbf{2}\,5\,8 \\ \hline 3\,4 \end{array}$$

Solution	How many voters voted in all? _____

Guided Instruction

| Problem 2 | The students are voting for a school color. The table shows the number of students who voted for each color. How many more votes did blue get than red? |

Color	Number of Votes
Blue	735
Green	402
Red	297
Yellow	156

You can subtract to find how many more.

Step 1   Subtract the ones.

Are 7 ones greater than 5 ones? _____

Do you need to regroup? _____

Regroup 3 tens and 5 ones as _____ tens and

_____ ones.

$$\begin{array}{r} 7\ 3\ \mathbf{5} \\ -\ 2\ 9\ \mathbf{7} \\ \hline \end{array}$$

Step 2   Subtract the tens.

Are 9 tens greater than 2 tens? _____

Do you need to regroup? _____

Regroup 7 hundreds and 2 tens as _____ hundreds

and _____ tens.

$$\begin{array}{r} {}^{2\ 15} \\ 7\ \cancel{3}\ \cancel{5} \\ -\ 2\ 9\ 7 \\ \hline 8 \end{array}$$

Step 3   Subtract the hundreds.

Are 2 hundreds greater than 6 hundreds? _____

Do you need to regroup? _____

The answer in subtraction is called the **difference**. ⟶

$$\begin{array}{r} {}^{6\ \ 12} \\ \cancel{7}\ \cancel{\cancel{3}}\ \cancel{5} \\ -\ 2\ 9\ 7 \\ \hline 3\ 8 \end{array}$$

| Solution | How many more votes did blue get than red? _____ |

Another Example

How many more votes did green get than yellow?
If one of the digits is zero, you can regroup in the
next greater place.

$$\begin{array}{r} {}^{3\ 10} \\ \cancel{4}\ \cancel{0}\ \cancel{2} \\ -\ 1\ 5\ 6 \\ \hline \_\ \_\ \_ \end{array}$$

Apply the GPS

Find each sum. Check your answers.

1.   196
      + 437

2.   438
      + 954

3.   672
      + 56

4.   508
      + 79

5.   836
      + 379

6. 709 + 98 = _____

7.   8
        2
        6
      + 9

8.   57
        23
      + 49

9.   16
        84
      + 37

Subtract. Check your answers.

10.   675
       − 127

11.   1,568
        − 219

12.   208
       − 79

13.   3,027
        − 854

14.   413
       − 306

15. 1,903 − 62 = _____

16.   548
       − 463

17.   950
       − 542

18.   500
       − 41

Write your answers to questions 19–21.

19. Janie wrote some pairs of numbers below. Which pair of numbers has the greatest difference? Explain your answer.

        23 and 19   2 and 14   57 and 51

_____

_____

20. Marcus is subtracting 100 from 8,016. He is writing the answer. What digit should be in the hundreds place? Explain your answer.

_____

_____

21. Lena was born in 1992. Her brother, Joe, was born five years before her. Her sister, Kim, was born nine years after Joe. In what years were Joe and Kim born?

_____

Directions: Choose the best answer for each question.
Circle the letter for the answer you have chosen.

1. At the Town Family Fair, 374 people arrived in the morning. Then 59 of the people left. Then 196 more people arrived in the afternoon. How many people were at the fair now?

    A. 119

    B. 271

    C. 511

    D. 629

2. The table below shows the monthly sales of Mill Town Garden Center.

Month	Number of Plants
June	639
July	815

    What is the difference between the number of plants sold in June and July?

    A. 1,454

    B. 224

    C. 186

    D. 176

3. Tia was born in 1989. Her sister, Nell, was born six years after her, and her brother, Lou, was born 12 years before Nell. In what years were Nell and Lou born?

    A. 1995 and 1983

    B. 1994 and 1982

    C. 1989 and 1977

    D. 1983 and 1971

 4. The table below shows the test scores of four students.

Name	Number of Points
Don	16
Suzi	14
Li-Wei	47
Neal	29

    Don, Suzi, and Neal found the total of their three scores. How many more points did they have together than Li-Wei?

    A. 106

    B. 59

    C. 22

    D. 12

Lesson 7 Estimate Sums and Differences

M4N2.b	Describe situations in which rounding numbers would be appropriate and determine whether to round to the nearest ten, hundred, or thousand.
M4N2.d	Represent the results of computation as a rounded number when appropriate and estimate a sum or difference by rounding numbers.
M4N7.d	Use mental math and estimation strategies to compute.
M4P1.d	Determine the most efficient way to solve a problem (mentally, paper/pencil, or calculator).

Rounding or front-end estimation can help to estimate sums and differences. Both methods give you numbers with more zeros that are easier to work with.

Guided Instruction

Problem 1

The distance from Atlanta to Omaha is 986 miles. The distance from Atlanta to Washington, D.C. is 608 miles. Using rounding, what is an estimate of how many fewer miles it is from Atlanta to Washington than it is to Omaha?

Use rounding to estimate the difference.

Step 1 First, round each number. To find easy numbers to work with, round to the greatest place.

9̶8̶6 rounded to the nearest hundred is 1,000

6̶0̶8 rounded to the nearest hundred is _____.

Step 2 Subtract in your head using the rounded numbers.

1,000 − 600 = _____

Solution What is the estimated difference in miles? _____

Guided Instruction

Problem 2

The distance from Atlanta to New York is 841 miles. The distance from New York to Boston is 206 miles. Using front-end estimation, what is an estimate of the total number of miles from Atlanta to New York to Boston?

Use front-end estimation to estimate the sum.

Step 1 Use the "front" digits. These are the digits in the greatest place.

8̲41 ⟶ 800   Use zeros for the other digits.

2̲06 ⟶ _____

Step 2 Add in your head using the front-end estimates.

800 + 200 = _____

Solution What is estimated total number of miles from Atlanta to New York to Boston? _____

Apply the GPS

Estimate each answer. Use rounding, and then use front-end estimation for each.

		Using Rounding	Using Front-end Estimation
1.	853 + 428	_____	_____
2.	967 − 785	_____	_____
3.	714 − 150	_____	_____
4.	503 + 576	_____	_____

Estimate to answer each problem. Use mental math, if you wish.

5. On Thursday, 461 parents came to see the students sing. On Friday, 638 parents came to see the students sing. Using rounding, what is an estimate of how many more parents came on Friday than on Thursday? _____

6. A bus driver drove 795 miles from Atlanta to Dallas. Then the bus driver drove 917 miles from Dallas to Chicago. Using front-end estimation, what is an estimate of the total number of miles the bus driver drove? _____

Use the table to solve problems 7 and 8.
Choose mental math or paper and pencil.

7. Using rounding, what is an estimate of how much shorter the Louisiana coastline is than the Florida coastline?

_____

Did you choose mental math or paper and pencil? Explain why.

_____

_____

Length of Coastlines

State	Miles
Florida	580
Louisiana	397
North Carolina	301
Virginia	112

8. Using front-end estimation, what is an estimate of total length in miles for the North Carolina and Virginia coastlines? _____

Did you choose mental math or paper and pencil? Explain why.

_____

_____

CRCT Practice **Directions: Choose the best answer for each question.**
Circle the letter for the answer you have chosen.

1. A bicycle shop fixed 389 bicycles last year and 527 bicycles this year. If you use rounding, which is the BEST estimate for the number of bicycles fixed in both years?

   A. 700

   B. 800

   C. 900

   D. 1,000

2. The table below shows the number of students in grade 3 and the number in grade 4.

Grade	Number of Students
Grade 3	115
Grade 4	231

   Using front-end estimation, estimate the total number of students in both grades.

   A. 100

   B. 200

   C. 300

   D. 400

3. Mei bought 650 feet of yarn. She used 214 feet of the yarn to make a hat. About how many feet of yarn does Mei have left?

   A. 900

   B. 800

   C. 500

   D. 300

4. The table below shows the number of points Bob, Donna, and Kyle scored on a computer game.

Name	Number of Points
Bob	831
Donna	709
Kyle	468

   Using front-end estimation, estimate how many fewer points Kyle has than Bob.

   A. 300

   B. 400

   C. 800

   D. 1,200

M4P1.c | Determine the operation(s) needed to solve a problem.
M4P1.d | Determine the most efficient way to solve a problem (mentally, paper/pencil, or calculator).

Choose a computation method to help you solve problems.

Guided Instruction

| **Problem** | Selena has 297 American dolls and 168 foreign dolls in her collection. What is the total number of dolls in Selena's collection? |

(U)nderstand the problem.

What do you need to find?

_____

(M)ake a plan.

Choose a method to find the answer.

Use **mental math** when you compute with basic facts or multiples of 10 or 100.

Use **paper and pencil** or **a calculator** when you need to regroup.

(S)olve the problem.

Add to find the total. Since you need to regroup more than once to find the total, use paper and pencil or a calculator.

Paper and pencil

$$\begin{array}{r} 297 \\ + 168 \\ \hline \end{array}$$

Calculator

2	9	7	+
1	6	8	=

How many dolls are in Selena's collection? _____

(C)heck your answer.

Subtract the number of American dolls from the total number of dolls. Check that the display shows the number of foreign dolls.

_____ − _____ = 168

Apply the GPS

Solve each problem. Choose mental math, paper and pencil, or a calculator.

Work Space

1. Tanya bought 4 sheets of postage stamps. There are 20 stamps on each sheet. How many stamps does Tanya have in all?

   _____ Method: _____

2. In August, Perry's Car Dealership sold 202 cars. In September, they sold 250 cars. How many cars did Perry's Car Dealership sell in both months?

   _____ Method: _____

3. There were 400 people at the football game on Saturday. On Sunday, there were 100 fewer people at the game than there were on Saturday. How many people were at the game on Sunday?

   _____ Method: _____

4. Cameron paid $497 for a digital camera and $119 for a DVD player. How much more did the camera cost than the DVD player?

   _____ Method: _____

5. How many sandwiches can you make with 18 slices of bread?

   _____ Method: _____

Directions: Choose the best answer for each question.
Circle the letter for the answer you have chosen.

1. When would it be best to use paper and pencil or a calculator to find a sum?

   A. when there are no regroupings

   B. when there are many regroupings

   C. when both addends are multiples of 10

   D. when each addend is less than 10

2. Use the data below.

   How much do two baseballs and one bat cost?

   A. $20

   B. $30

   C. $40

   D. $50

3. Which would be the best method to use to find 700 + 700?

   A. paper and pencil

   B. calculator

   C. mental math

   D. computer

4. Students at Williamsville Elementary School held an election for school president. Young Lee received 316 votes, and Mark received 403 votes. How many more votes did Mark receive than Young Lee?

   A. 73 votes

   B. 87 votes

   C. 719 votes

   D. 819 votes

Applying Concepts

Directions: Choose the best answer for each question.
Circle the letter for the answer you have chosen.

1. The Bank of America Plaza Building in Atlanta is 1,023 feet tall. What is the expanded form of the number 1,023?

   A. 1,000 + 3 + 2

   B. 1,000 + 20 + 3

   C. 10,000 + 2 + 3

   D. 10,000 + 20 + 3

2. What is the missing number at the arrow?

   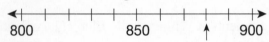

   A. 885

   B. 880

   C. 870

   D. 865

3. Find the difference.

   $$\begin{array}{r} 921 \\ -\ 357 \\ \hline \end{array}$$

   A. 564

   B. 636

   C. 674

   D. 1,278

 4. Which group does NOT show the numbers ordered from greatest to least?

   A. 9,215, 9,198, 9,197

   B. 6,329, 6,048, 6,012

   C. 4,391, 4,385, 4,372

   D. 2,594, 2,503, 2,512

 5. The table below shows the number of new students in three elementary schools.

New City Elementary Schools	
School Name	Number of New Students
Alton	151
Grove	117
Parkside	308

Using front-end estimation, estimate the total number of new students in all three schools.

   A. 100

   B. 200

   C. 500

   D. 700

     Measuring Up® to the Georgia Performance Standards

6. The students at West School chose which meals they wanted at lunch. Their choices were pasta, salad, or a sandwich. There were 375 students. 130 students chose pasta. 46 students chose salad. How many students chose a sandwich?

   A. 199

   B. 201

   C. 245

   D. 551

7. The distance between Atlanta and Chicago is 674 miles. What is 674 rounded to the nearest ten?

   A. 700

   B. 680

   C. 670

   D. 600

8. Oscar changed the 5 in the number 75,269 to a 3. How did he change the value?

   A. increased by 20,000

   B. increased by 2,000

   C. decreased by 20,000

   D. decreased by 2,000

9. What is the value of the underlined digit in 9,673?

   A. 6

   B. 60

   C. 600

   D. 6,000

10. Which number completes the pattern?

    1, 6, 11, ___, 21

    A. 12

    B. 13

    C. 15

    D. 16

11. In the following story problem, select the BEST method for solving it:

    At Ace Shipping, the company had 427 boxes in a garage. The workers put 319 of the boxes on a truck. Then they brought 56 more boxes into the garage. How many boxes are in the garage now?

    A. Add 427 and 319, then add 56 to that answer.

    B. Add 427 and 319, then subtract 56 from that answer.

    C. Subtract 319 from 427, then add 56 to that answer.

    D. Subtract 319 from 427, then subtract 56 from that answer.

12. The table below shows the height of four mountains.

Name	Height in Feet
Marcy	5,344
Rogers	5,729
Spruce Knob	4,862
Washington	6,288

Which is the height of Spruce Knob Mountain rounded to the nearest hundred?

A. 6,300 feet

B. 4,900 feet

C. 4,860 feet

D. 4,800 feet

13. What is the sum of 39 and 85?

A. 125

B. 124

C. 114

D. 46

14. At Thursday's concert, 586 people attended. At Friday's concert, 825 people attended. Using rounding, what is an estimate of the total number of people who attended for both days?

A. 200

B. 300

C. 1,300

D. 1,400

15. This number 800,000 + 5,000 + 200 + 10 + 4 is written in expanded form. Which is the number in word form?

A. eight hundred five thousand, two hundred fourteen

B. eight hundred thousand, fifty-two hundred fourteen

C. eight thousand, five hundred, two fourteen

D. eighty-five thousand, two hundred forty

16. The table below lists the populations of three counties in Georgia in 2003.

County	Number of People
Baldwin	44,953
Camden	45,470
Jackson	46,998

In Camden County, 4 hundred people moved away in the year 2004. What was the new number of people in Camden County?

A. 41,470

B. 44,453

C. 45,070

D. 46,958

17. The table lists the number of pages in four books.

Book Title	Number of Pages
Amazon River	921
Great Mountains	745
Lions of Africa	408
Sea Explorations	419

Which two books have the greatest difference in number of pages?

A. *Amazon River* and *Lions of Africa*

B. *Amazon River* and *Great Mountains*

C. *Amazon River* and *Sea Explorations*

D. *Great Mountains* and *Lions of Africa*

18. For which problem would you probably use mental math to find the answer?

A. Wes biked 16 miles yesterday and 31 miles today. How many more miles did he bike today?

B. Belin babysat 2 times last week. The first time she earned $20 and the second time she earned $30. How much did she earn in all?

C. Derek waited on 41 diners at dinner and 29 diners at lunch. How many more diners did he wait on at dinner?

D. Liz's school has 406 students. Larry's school has 329 students. How many more students are in Liz's school?

19. Use mental math to find the sum.

$$\begin{array}{r} 2{,}527 \\ +\,1{,}373 \\ \hline \end{array}$$

A. 1,246

B. 3,890

C. 3,900

D. 3,990

20. Which number has a 3 in the ten thousands place?

A. 123,407

B. 274,365

C. 381,659

D. 537,428

21. Erica made the table below to show the number of books in three libraries.

Library	Number of Books
East Hill	25,410
Flores	?
North Hill	14,302

Flores Library has 4 thousand more books than North Hill Library. Which is the number of books that Flores Library has?

A. 10,302

B. 18,302

C. 29,410

D. 53,302

Lesson 9 Explore Multiples and Factors

Focus on GPS

M4N3	Students will solve problems involving multiplication of 2–3 digit numbers by 1–2 digit numbers.
M4P3	Students will use the language of mathematics to express ideas precisely.
M4P5	Students will create and use pictures, manipulatives, models, and symbols to organize, record, and communicate mathematical ideas.

You can use equal groups to help you understand multiplication.

Multiplication is an operation in which equal groups are combined.

Multiplication Word and Definition		Example
Product	the answer in multiplication	6 × 3 = 18 ◄——— 18 is the product
Factor	a number that is multiplied to give a product	6 × 3 = 18 6 and 3 are factors of 18.
Multiple	the product of a number and any other whole number	3, 6, 9, 12, 15, and 18 are some multiples of 3.

Guided Instruction

Problem	Ron has 6 boxes of toy planes. Each box has 3 planes. How many toy planes does Ron have in all?

Use models in groups and skip counting to help multiply.

Step 1 Decide if you are combining equal groups.

Ron has equal groups of planes, so you can multiply.

How many planes are in each equal group? _____

Step 2 Use models or skip counting to help multiply.

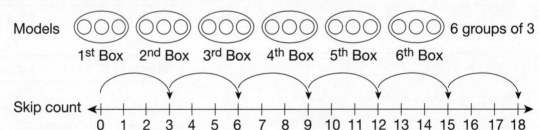

The numbers you say in skip counting by threes 6 times are

___3___ , ___6___ ,_____, _____, _____, and _____.

Step 3 Complete a multiplication sentence.

6	×	3	=	_____
number of groups		number in each group		number in all

Solution	How many toy planes does Ron have in all? _____

Apply the GPS

Write three multiples of each number.

1. Multiples of 4

_____, _____, _____

2. Multiples of 7

_____, _____, _____

3. Multiples of 5

_____, _____, _____

Write an even number between 30 and 40 that is a multiple of each number.

4. A multiple of 9

_____

5. A multiple of 6

_____

6. A multiple of 8

_____

Write each product.

7. $4 \times 2 =$ _____

8. $7 \times 3 =$ _____

9. $5 \times 6 =$ _____

Solve each problem. Write a multiplication sentence that solves the problem.

10. Thea has 5 packs of tomatoes. Each pack has 3 tomatoes. How many tomatoes does Thea have in all? _____ tomatoes

_____ $\times$ _____ = _____

11. Each table in the classroom has 6 chairs. There are 4 tables. How many chairs are at the tables? _____ chairs

_____ $\times$ _____ = _____

12. Each basket on the table has 4 apples in it. There are 3 baskets. How many apples are in the baskets in all? _____ apples

_____ $\times$ _____ = _____

13. There are 8 teams in the town swim league. There are 5 swimmers on each team. How many swimmers are in the league?

_____ swimmers

_____ $\times$ _____ = _____

Write the answer to each question. Explain your method.

14. Kevin got $7 each week for chores. There were 4 weeks this month. What is the total amount that Kevin got for chores this month?

_____

15. The students got on an empty bus. Each seat on the bus can hold 2 students. The students filled 8 seats in all. How many students were seated on the bus?

_____

CRCT Practice

Directions: Choose the best answer for each question.
Circle the letter for the answer you have chosen.

1. Which number between 25 and 35 is a multiple of 6?

   A. 26

   B. 30

   C. 33

   D. 34

 2. Which number is NOT a multiple of 12?

   A. 12

   B. 36

   C. 52

   D. 72

3. If you were counting by 3s, what would be the next number after 210?

   A. 212

   B. 213

   C. 214

   D. 240

4. Kelli is skip counting on a number line to find 3 groups of 4. Which number should Kelli say next in the skip count?

   A. 4

   B. 11

   C. 12

   D. 13

 5. Harry put stamps into groups of 2. He made 4 groups of stamps. Which number sentence correctly represents this picture?

   □□ □□ □□ □□

   A. $2 \times 4 = 8$

   B. $12 - 4 = 8$

   C. $4 \times 4 = 16$

   D. $8 \times 2 = 16$

         Measuring Up® to the Georgia Performance Standards

Lesson 10 Explore Prime and Composite Numbers

M4N3   Students will solve problems involving multiplication of 2–3 digit numbers by 1–2 digit numbers.
M4P2   Students will investigate, develop, and evaluate mathematical arguments.

You can use multiples to help find prime numbers and composite numbers.

A **prime number** is a whole number whose only factors are 1 and itself.

A **composite number** is a whole number that has more than two factors.

Any number that is a multiple of another number is a composite number.

Guided Instruction

Problem

Leo wants to find a number that has no factors other than itself and 1. He wants to find all of these numbers from 1 to 40. Which are the prime numbers between 1 and 40?

Use multiples and skip counting to help find prime numbers.

Step 1   Make a list of all the whole numbers from 2 to 40.

Mathematicians agree that 1 is neither prime nor composite.

> 2   3   4   5   6   7   8   9   10   11   12   13   14
> 15   16   17   18   19   20   21   22   23   24   25   26   27
> 28   29   30   31   32   33   34   35   36   37   38   39   40

Step 2   Find the first number whose only factors are 1 and itself − a prime.

The number 2 has no factors other than itself and 1. $1 \times 2 = 2$

Circle the 2 as a prime number. Then cross out its multiples.

Any multiple of 2 has more than 2 factors, so it is a composite number. $2 \times 2 = 4$ and $1 \times 4 = 4$, so 4 is a composite number.

> ②   3   ~~4~~   5   ~~6~~   7   ~~8~~   9   ~~10~~   11   ~~12~~   13   ~~14~~
> 15   ~~16~~   17   ~~18~~   19   ~~20~~   21   ~~22~~   23   ~~24~~   25   ~~26~~   27
> ~~28~~   29   ~~30~~   31   ~~32~~   33   ~~34~~   35   ~~36~~   37   ~~38~~   39   ~~40~~

Find the next number whose only factors are 1 and itself.

The number 3 is the next prime.

Circle the 3. Cross out all of its multiples. The multiples of 3 are 6, 9, 12, 15, 18, 21, 24, 27, 30, _____, _____, _____, _____, _____, _____.

Repeat for each next prime. All numbers left are prime numbers.

Solution

Which are the prime numbers between 1 and 40?
2, 3, 5, 7, 11, 13, 17, 19, _____, _____, _____, _____

Apply the GPS

Write _prime_ or _composite_ for each number.

1. 4

_____

2. 39

_____

3. 23

_____

Which is the prime number in each group? Write the number.

4. 12, 17, 18, 21

_____

5. 34, 31, 30, 27

_____

6. 4, 5, 9, 10

_____

Which is NOT a prime number in each group? Write the number.

7. 2, 3, 14, 19

_____

8. 40, 41, 43, 47

_____

9. 37, 29, 27, 23

_____

Solve each problem.

10. Lyn is thinking of a prime number between 10 and 20. The number that is one greater than Lyn's number is a composite number with 9 as one of its factors. Which prime number is Lyn thinking of? _____

11. Ed is thinking of a composite number. It is between 41 and 50. It has 8 as one of its factors. Which composite number is Ed thinking of? _____

Write the answer to each question. Explain how you found your answer.

12. Are there any even numbers greater than 2 that are prime numbers? How do you know? _____

_____

13. Dina says that 9 is a prime number. Is she correct? Use multiplication to explain why or why not. _____

_____

14. Find all the prime numbers from 50 to 60. Show and explain your work.

_____

_____

_____

CRCT Practice

Directions: Choose the best answer for each question. Circle the letter for the answer you have chosen.

 1. Which is NOT a prime number?

    A. 2

    B. 6

    C. 7

    D. 13

2. The table below shows how many cans each student brought for recycling.

Name	Number of Cans
Cora	17
Dave	19
Luz	11
Toshi	18

Who brought a number of cans that is a composite number?

    A. Cora

    B. Dave

    C. Luz

    D. Toshi

3. Which shows a prime number of squares?

    A.

    B.

    C.

    D.

 4. Lily wants to find if 49 is a prime number or a composite number. Which shows that 49 is a composite number?

    A. $7 \times 7 = 49$

    B. $4 + 9 = 13$

    C. $9 - 4 = 5$

    D. $4 \times 9 = 36$

Lesson 11 Use Properties of Multiplication

You can use multiplication properties to help you find products.

Associative Property	The way factors are grouped does not change the product.	$(5 \times 2) \times 4 = 5 \times (2 \times 4)$
Commutative Property	Changing the order of the factors does not change the product.	$2 \times 4 = 8$ $4 \times 2 = 8$
Distributive Property	You can multiply a factor by another factor renamed as addends. Multiplying by each addend does not change the product.	$4 \times 7 = 4 \times (5 + 2)$ $= (4 \times 5) + (4 \times 2)$

Guided Instruction

Problem Leon put 9 muffins on each of 3 plates. How many muffins in all did Leon put on the plates?

Use the distributive property of multiplication.

Step 1 Write a number sentence to show the factors.

3 × 9 = ?

Step 2 Rename a factor as addends that may be easier to work with.

3 × 9 = ?

3 × (5 + 4) = ?

Step 3 Now multiply the factor by each addend. Then add.

(3 × 5) + (3 × 4)

15 + 12 = _____

Solution How many muffins in all did Leon put on the plates? _____.

Another Example

| Use the Associative Property to find the product of 3 factors. | Eli put 3 boxes on each of 5 tables. He put 2 cans in each box.
 $3 \times 5 \times 2 = (2 \times 5) \times 3$
 $10 \times 3 = $ _____ |

Apply the GPS

Complete each number sentence using the associative property. Find each product.

1. 2 × 4 × 5 = _____

(_____ × _____) × _____ = _____

2. 3 × 6 × 2 = _____

(_____ × _____) × _____ = _____

Complete each number sentence using the commutative property. Find each product.

3. 6 × 7 = _____

_____ × _____ = _____

4. 8 × 3 = _____

_____ × _____ = _____

Complete each number sentence using the distributive property. Find each product.

5. 4 × 9 = _____

_____ × (_____ + _____) = _____

6. 6 × 8 = _____

_____ × (_____ + _____) = _____

Write the answer to each question.

7. Miko put 6 plates on each of 2 tables. She put 2 apples on each plate. How many apples did Miko put on the plates in all? _____

8. Yuri used the distributive property to write a number sentence another way.

$$9 \times 6 = (2 + 7) \times 6$$

What is another way to use the distributive property for 9 × 6?

_____

What is the product? _____

9. Jo used the distributive property to help her multiply. She wrote this sentence to help.

$$(2 \times 4) + (2 \times 3) =$$

What is a multiplication sentence Jo could be working on? Explain your answer.

_____ × _____ =

_____

_____

CRCT Practice Directions: Choose the best answer for each question. Circle the letter for the answer you have chosen.

Use the table below to answer questions 1 and 2.

Bowling Leagues

League	Number of Teams	Number of Players on Each Team
A	5	4
B	6	3

1. Which number sentence can be used to find the total number of players in League A?

   A. $5 + 4$

   B. 6×3

   C. 5×4

   D. $4 + 3$

 2. Which number sentence shows two ways to find the total number of players in League B?

   A. $6 + 3 = (2 + 3) + (3 + 3)$

   B. $6 \times 3 = 3 \times 6$

   C. $5 \times 4 = (5 \times 2) + (5 \times 2)$

   D. $4 + 3 = 3 + 4$

3. What is the correct product:

   $$(3 \times 8) \times 2 \ ?$$

   A. 14

   B. 22

   C. 26

   D. 48

4. Which of the following shows the associative property of multiplication?

   A. $7 \times 8 = 8 \times 7$

   B. $(3 \times 9) \times 2 = 3 \times (9 \times 2)$

   C. $6 = 6 \times 1$

   D. $4 \times 5 = (4 \times 2) + (4 \times 3)$

 5. Tim wrote $(3 + 4) \times 6$ to multiply 7×6. Selena said she can use another way to multiply 7×6. Which number sentence is true?

   A. $(3 + 4) \times 6 = (2 \times 5) \times 6$

   B. $(3 + 4) \times 6 = (2 \times 5) + 6$

   C. $(3 + 4) \times 6 = (2 + 5) \times 6$

   D. $(3 + 4) \times 6 = (2 + 5) + 6$

Lesson 12 Multiply by a 1-Digit Factor

M4N3 Students will solve problems involving multiplication of 2-3 digit numbers by 1-2 digit numbers.

M4P5 Students will create and use pictures, manipulatives, models, and symbols to organize, record, and communicate mathematical ideas.

You can use an array to multiply two factors and show how the equal groups are arranged. An **array** is a set of items arranged in rows and columns. The number of rows in an array shows one factor in the problem. The number of items in each row, or the number of columns, shows the other factor.

Guided Instruction

| **Problem** | A parking lot has 3 rows. There are 14 cars parked in each row. What is the total number of cars parked in the lot? |

Use an array and the distributive property to multiply a 2-digit number by a 1-digit number.

Step 1 Think of the ones and tens in the 2-digit factor. $14 = 4 + 10$

Think: $\begin{array}{r} 14 \\ \times\ \underline{\ 3} \end{array}$ ← 3 groups of 4 ones   And $\begin{array}{r} 14 \\ \times\ \underline{\ 3} \end{array}$ ← 3 groups of 1 ten

$3 \times 14 = (3 \times 4) + (3 \times 10)$

Step 2 Draw an array.

Show the groups of one. Show the groups of ten.

Show the items in rows and columns.

rows go across →

3 rows of 4   3 rows of 10

How many items are in 3 rows of 4? _____

How many items are in 3 rows of 10? _____

Step 3 Add the numbers in the arrays. $12 + $ _____ $= $ _____

Write the product. $3 \times 14 = $ _____

| **Solution** | What is the total number of cars parked in the lot? _____ |

Apply the GPS

Write the multiplication sentence and product that each array represents.

1.

_____

2.

_____

3.

_____

Find the product. Use arrays if you wish.

4. 17
   $\times\ 4$

5. 19
   $\times\ 3$

6. 25
   $\times\ 7$

7. 34
   $\times\ 2$

8. 18
   $\times\ 5$

9. $6 \times 13 =$ _____

10. $20 \times 7 =$ _____

11. $3 \times 40 =$ _____

Solve each problem. Draw an array that can be used to solve the problem.

12. Mrs. Lopez is putting sheets of paper into rows to help find the total. There are 4 different colors of paper. Mrs. Lopez has 16 sheets of each color. How many sheets of paper does she have in all? _____

13. Some friends planted 13 trees in each row at a farm. They made 2 rows of trees. What was the total number of trees planted? _____

Explain why using an array can be helpful when you use the distributive property to multiply.

_____

_____

_____

_____

   Measuring Up® to the Georgia Performance Standards

CRCT Practice Directions: Choose the best answer for each question. Circle the letter for the answer you have chosen.

1. There are 30 crates on a truck. There are 4 milk jugs in each crate. How many milk jugs are in the crates?

   A. 34

   B. 120

   C. 180

   D. 340

 2. Which number sentence correctly represents this picture?

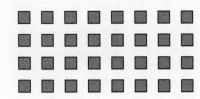

   A. $4 + 4 + 4 + 4 = 16$

   B. $4 \times 4 = 16$

   C. $4 \times 8 = 32$

   D. $8 \times 8 = 64$

 3. Shelly baked pies for a bake sale. She baked 4 pies during each part of the day—the morning, afternoon, and evening. Then she baked 2 more pies the next day. What method can you use to find the number of pies Shelly baked in all?

   A. Add 4 pies to three pies, then add 2 more pies

   B. Add 4 pies to 2 pies, then multiply by three.

   C. Multiply 4 pies by three, then multiply by 2 more pies.

   D. Multiply 4 pies by three, then add 2 pies.

4. What is the product of 4×16?

   A. 42

   B. 60

   C. 64

   D. 96

Lesson 13 | Multiply by a 2-Digit Factor

M4N3   Students will solve problems involving multiplication of 2–3 digit numbers by 1–2 digit numbers.

M4P4   Students will understand how mathematical ideas interconnect and build on one another and apply mathematics in other content areas.

M4P5   Students will create and use pictures, manipulatives, models, and symbols to organize, record, and communicate mathematical ideas.

You can use area models and facts to help multiply larger numbers.

An **area model** is a rectangular grid formed from unit squares. The numbers of rows and columns in the area model show the factors you are multiplying. The total number of unit squares in the area model is the product of the factors.

Guided Instruction

| **Problem** | At Pine Tree Farm, there are 15 rows of pine trees. Each row has 24 trees. What is the total number of pine trees at the farm? |

Use an area model and the distributive property to find the product.

Step 1   You can think of the ones place and the tens place to multiply.

Think: $\begin{array}{r} 24 \\ \times\ 15 \end{array}$ ◄— **5** groups of **4** $\begin{array}{r} 24 \\ \times\ 15 \end{array}$ ◄— **10** groups of **4**

                                5 groups of **20**   **10** groups of **20**

Step 2   Draw an area model on a grid to show the groups of ones and tens.

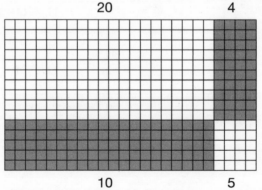

10 × 20 = →
200

5 × 20 = →
_____

10 × 4 =
40

5 × 4 =
_____

20   4

10   5

Step 3   Add the products of each section to find the product.

$$\begin{array}{r} 20 \\ 100 \\ 40 \\ +\ 200 \\ \hline \end{array}$$

| **Solution** | What is the total number of pine trees? _____ |

Write the number sentences and find the product that the area model represents.

1. 23 × 16

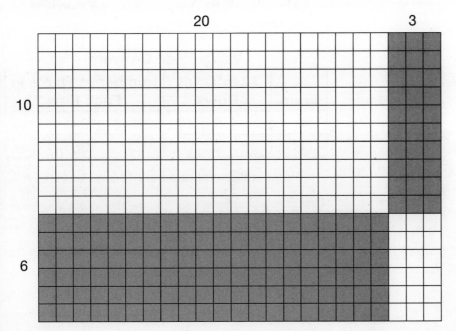

_____6_____ × _____3_____ = _____18_____

_____ × _____ = _____

_____ × _____ = _____

_____ × _____ = _____

_____

_____

_____

+ _____

_____

Find the product. Use area models and facts you know, if you wish.

2. 12 × 17 = _____

3. 25 × 14 = _____

4. 11 × 29 = _____

5.   26
       × 18

6.   19
       × 13

7.   100
       × 21

8.   34
       × 23

9.   45
       × 16

Solve each problem.

10. Leo has 23 kinds of stamps. He has 12 of each kind of stamp. Draw an area model on another sheet. How many stamps does he have in all?

_____

_____

11. Explain how you can use sections in an area model to multiply larger factors.

_____

_____

_____

CRCT Practice **Directions: Choose the best answer for each question.**
Circle the letter for the answer you have chosen.

1. Find the product:

   $$12 \times 16 = \ ?$$

   A. 28

   B. 96

   C. 114

   D. 192

2. Misha's class made posters for the school play. Each student made 16 posters. There were 29 students in the class. How many posters did the class make?

   A. 484

   B. 464

   C. 95

   D. 77

3. Which number sentence does NOT show another method to solve:

   $$25 \times 12 = \ ?$$

   A. $(25 \times 2) + (25 \times 10)$

   B. $(25 \times 4) + (5 \times 8)$

   C. $(20 \times 12) + (5 \times 12)$

   D. $(5 \times 12) + (5 \times 12)$

4. The table below shows the rows and columns of rose plants on two farms.

   Valley Rose Growers

Farm	Number of Rows	Number of Plants in Each Row
A	5	124
B	4	135

   What is the total number of plants at Farm A?

   A. 620

   B. 540

   C. 259

   D. 129

5. Mr. Chen bought 13 cartons of nails for his store. Each carton had 42 boxes of nails in it. Which number sentence shows how many boxes of nails he bought in all?

   A. $42 - 13$

   B. $42 \div 13$

   C. 13×42

   D. $13 + 42$

Lesson 14 Estimate Products

M4N7.d   Use mental math and estimation strategies to compute.

M4P1.a   Solve non-routine word problems using the strategies of work backwards, use or make a table, and make an organized list as well as all strategies learned in previous grades.

You can use rounding and estimation when an exact product is not needed.

You can also estimate to check if a product makes sense. Two methods of estimating are rounding and front-end estimation.

Guided Instruction

Problem 1

Daniel drove from Georgia to Colorado in 21 hours. He drove 65 miles each hour. About how many miles did Daniel drive?

Use rounding and mental math to estimate the product.

Step 1   Round each factor. You can round to the nearest ten.

Think: 21 ⟶ 21 rounded to the nearest ten is _____.

$\times$ 65 ⟶ 65 rounded to the nearest ten is _____.

Step 2   Use mental math to multiply with the rounded factors.

You can use a multiplication fact to help.

Think: $2 \times 7 = 14$ and $20 \times 70 = 1,400$

Solution   About how many miles did Daniel drive? about _____

Guided Instruction

Problem 2

Flo drives 129 miles total for one round trip to visit her sister. She has made 4 round trips this month. About how many miles has Flo driven to visit her sister this month?

Use front-end estimation and mental math.

Step 1   Use front-end estimation. Estimate using just the greater factor. Remember: The "front" digits are the digits in the greatest place.

Think: 129 ⟶ 100   Keep the front digit and use zeros.

$\times$ 4

Step 2   Use mental math to multiply with the front-end estimate.

Think: $100 \times 4 =$ _____

Solution   About how many miles has Flo driven to visit her sister?

about _____

Apply the GPS

Estimate each product. Use rounding to the nearest ten for each factor.

1. 74 × 18 = _____

2. 32
×26
_____

3. 129
× 13
_____

4. 85
× 47
_____

Estimate each product. Use front-end estimation for the greater factor in each.

5. 136 × 9 = _____

6. 207
× 4
_____

7. 96
× 12
_____

8. 5
× 71
_____

Estimate to answer each problem. Use mental math, if you wish.

9. Oscar trained to run in a big race. He ran 46 laps around the track each day. He ran laps each day for two weeks. Each week has 7 days. Using rounding to the nearest ten, about how many laps did Oscar run all together in the two weeks?

about _____

10. A bus driver drove 353 miles from Detroit to Milwaukee. Then he drove back the same number of miles. He did the same thing for two more days. Using front-end estimation, about how many miles did the driver drive in the three days?

about _____

Use the table to solve problems 11–13. Use mental math, if you wish.

Our Stamp Books

Name	Number of Rows	Stamps in Each Row
Clara	5	67
Hamid	43	75
Louis	18	32
Mori	7	119

11. Using rounding, about how many stamps does Louis have? about _____

12. Using front-end estimation for both factors, what is an estimate of the total number of stamps Hamid has? _____

13. Using front-end estimation, about how many stamps does Mori have?

_____

Explain how you can find a different estimate by rounding.

_____

_____

CRCT Practice

Directions: Choose the best answer for each question. Circle the letter for the answer you have chosen.

 1. Last week, Kevin drove 73 miles to visit his brother. Then he drove back the same number of miles. He did the same thing this week. About how many miles did Kevin drive to visit his brother in the two weeks?

A. 70

B. 140

C. 280

D. 400

2. Drew and Patty made the table below to help them count their stickers.

Name	Number of Rows	Number of Stickers in Each Row
Drew	45	19
Patty	37	12

Using rounding, estimate the total number of stickers Patty has.

A. 100

B. 400

C. 1,000

D. 1,400

3. At Hill School, 112 new books arrived for each grade: grade 2, grade 3, and grade 4. Which shows one way to find about how many books arrived at the school in all?

A. 3×100

B. 4×100

C. $117 - 3$

D. $(117 + 3) \times 4$

 4. The table below shows a record of Perry's driving trip.

Day	Hours Driven	Speed
1	8	65 miles per hour
2	7	55 miles per hour

Which is the BEST estimate of about how many miles Perry drove on Day 1?

A. 70

B. 420

C. 560

D. 800

Lesson 15 Problem-Solving Strategy: Make a Table

M4N3   Students will solve problems involving multiplication of 2–3 digit numbers by 1–2 digit numbers.
M4P1.a   Solve non-routine word problems using the strategies of work backwards, use or make a table, and make an organized list as well as all strategies learned in previous grades.

You can make a table to help you solve problems that use multiplication.

Guided Instruction

Problem

Tickets for a nature show cost the same for each person. Tickets for 9 people cost $72. 13 tickets cost $104 and 15 tickets cost $120. There are 17 people in Velma's group. What would be the total cost for 17 people?

Understand the problem.

What do I know? _____

_____

What do I need to find out? _____

Make a plan.

You can make a table to help you find a pattern.

Solve the problem.

Make a table. Look at the table to find a pattern.

Cost of Nature Show Tickets

Number of People	Total Amount
9	$72
13	$104
15	$120
17	$____

You know that each ticket costs the same. How can you use multiplication to get from the number in the left column to the number in the right column?

_____

_____

The rule for the table is to **multiply by $_____.**

Check your answer.

Use the rule to check your answer. Write number sentences.

_____

Apply the GPS

Solve each problem. Make a table, if you wish.

1. Each runner in a race is given the same number of bottles of water. For 12 runners, the total number of bottles is 84. For 14 runners, the total number is 98. For 17 runners, the total number is 119. What is the total number of bottles for 19 runners? _____

2. The cost of a roller-coaster ride ticket is the same for each rider. For 9 people, the total amount for tickets is $27. For 13 people, the total amount is $36. For 16 people, the total amount is $48. There are 18 people in Ron's group. What would be the total amount for 18 people? _____

3. Theo is starting a new job on May 1. He will make $15 each day cleaning up lawns. He will work every day. Theo wants to earn $210 to buy a bicycle. On what date will he have earned $210? _____

4. Judy is making hats to sell. Each day she makes 4 hats. Judy has a total of 52 hats after 13 days. How many hats will she have after 16 days? _____

Write the rule for each table. Find the missing number.

5. What can you do to each "In" number to get its "Out" number?

In	Out
6	36
14	___
30	180
40	240

Rule: _____

Missing Number: _____

6. Corey made this table to show how many minutes he practiced the violin.

Practice Violin	Week 1	Week 2	Week 3	Week 4
Minutes	35	70	___	140

Rule: _____

_____

Missing Number: _____

Use the table to solve problems 7–9.

7. What is the rule for getting from number A to number B?

_____

8. Use the rule to find the pair of numbers that is missing. _____

9. Is this the rule for the table? Explain why or why not.

_____

A	B
6	54
7	63
8	72
10	90

CRCT Practice   **Directions: Choose the best answer for each question.**
Circle the letter for the answer you have chosen.

 1. Marcus is starting to read a book. Each day he reads 9 pages. If on the fifteenth day, Marcus reads a total of 135 pages of the book, how many pages would he read in all on the seventeenth day?

A. 1,215

B. 176

C. 153

D. 144

 2. Look at the pairs of numbers in the table below.

In	Out
9	54
11	66
13	78
15	90

Which pair of numbers would NOT belong in the table if more rows were added?

A   10 and 60

B. 12 and 72

C. 16 and 80

D. 17 and 102

3. Look at the pairs of numbers in the table below.

In	Out
8	72
20	180
35	315
50	450

What can you do to each "In" number to get its "Out" number?

A. add 64

B. add 72

C. multiply by 7

D. multiply by 9

4. Yuki made this table to show how many laps she was able to run around the track each week. Complete the table.

Week	Week 1	Week 2	Week 3	Week 4
Number of Laps	24	48	___	96

A. 82

B. 72

C. 64

D. 54

Directions: Choose the best answer for each question.
Circle the letter for the answer you have chosen.

1. What is the missing factor?

$$12 \times \boxed{} = 144$$

   A. 11

   B. 12

   C. 13

   D. 132

2. The community garden is having a planting day. There will be 4 rows in the garden. Each row will have 6 vegetable plants and 3 flower plants. How many plants will be in the garden in all?

   A. 72

   B. 36

   C. 30

   D. 13

3. Which number is a multiple of 9?

   A. 19

   B. 29

   C. 36

   D. 39

4. Which is a prime number?

   A. 23

   B. 34

   C. 39

   D. 40

5. The table below shows the number of trucks at two parking lots.

Lot	Number of Rows	Number of Trucks in Each Row
Main Street	24	46
Vine Road	32	15

   Using rounding, estimate the total number of trucks at the Vine Road lot.

   A. 50

   B. 300

   C. 600

   D. 1,000

6. Which number sentence correctly represents this picture?

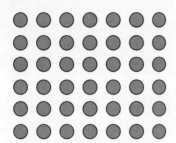

A. $6 \times 7 = 42$

B. $7 \times 7 = 49$

C. $7 + 6 = 13$

D. $6 + 6 + 6 + 6 + 6 + 6 = 36$

7. What is the correct product:

$$(4 \times 5) \times 4 \quad ?$$

A. 13

B. 24

C. 36

D. 80

8. The city held a basketball game day for students. Each basketball team had 5 players. There were 37 teams. How many players were there in all?

A. 385

B. 185

C. 50

D. 42

9. Annie made 8 necklaces. She used 73 beads to make each necklace. About how many beads did Annie use in all?

A. 800

B. 640

C. 560

D. 80

10. Carlos is starting a bicycle trip. Each day he rides 8 miles. In seventeen days, Carlos rides a total of 136 miles. How many miles will he ride in all in nineteen days?

A. 1,088

B. 180

C. 152

D. 144

11. Which operations make the following equation true?

$$(7 \boxed{} 2) + (5 \boxed{} 3) = 29$$

A. $\times, +$

B. $+, \times$

C. $+, +$

D. $\times, \times$

12. There are 40 cars on the roller coaster ride. There are four riders in each car. How many riders are on the roller coaster?

    A. 440

    B. 160

    C. 80

    D. 44

13. If you were counting by 4s, what would be the next number after 188?

    A. 189

    B. 191

    C. 192

    D. 228

14. Which number sentence is true?

    A. $9 \times 4 = 4 \times 9$

    B. $9 - 4 = 4 - 9$

    C. $9(4 + 9) = 36$

    D. $9(4 + 9) = 4 \times 9$

15. What can you do to each "In" number to get its "Out" number?

In	Out
6	42
15	105
30	210
40	280

    A. add 36

    B. add 180

    C. multiply by 6

    D. multiply by 7

 16. Which is NOT a prime number?

    A. 2

    B. 3

    C. 7

    D. 9

17. Look at the table below.

Hill Top Milk Farm

Size of Crate	Number of Crates	Number of Cartons in Each Crate
Large	27	18
Small	37	14

What is the total number of cartons the small crates can hold?

A. 518

B. 486

C. 440

D. 51

18. Which property of multiplication does $9 \times 1 = 9$ show?

A. property of one

B. property of zero

C. distributive property

D. associative property

19. Use the rule to find the pair of numbers that is missing.

24		32
6		8

A. 30, 7

B. 28, 7

C. 25, 7

D. 25, 5

20. Complete the statement:

$$(8 + 6) \times 2 = ?$$

A. $(7 + 7) \times 2$

B. $(7 + 2) \times 7$

C. $8 + (6 \times 2)$

D. $8 \times (2 + 6)$

21. Find the product:

$$17 \times 13 = ?$$

A. 28

B. 32

C. 131

D. 221

Chapter 3

Focus on GPS

Lesson 16 Relate Multiplication and Division

M4N4.a	Know the division facts with understanding and fluency.
M4P1.b	Solve single and multi-step routine word problems related to all appropriate fourth-grade math standards.
M4P4	Students will understand how mathematical ideas interconnect and build on one another and apply mathematics in other content areas.

You can use multiplication facts to find related division facts. **Related facts** are multiplication and division facts that are in the same fact family. **A fact family** is a group of multiplication and division facts that use the same set of whole numbers.

Guided Instruction

Problem 1 The 28 children at the picnic will be placed in 4 equal teams. How many children will there be on each team?

Step 1 The problem is about separating equal groups, so you can divide. Write a division sentence for the problem.

$$28 \div 4 = ?$$

number in all	number of groups	number in each group

Step 2 Find a related multiplication fact for the division sentence.

$$4 \times \underline{\hspace{1cm}} = 28$$

number of groups	number in each group	number in all

Step 3 Use the related fact to complete the division sentence.

$$4 \times 7 = 28 \qquad\qquad 28 \div 4 = \underline{\hspace{1cm}}$$

Solution How many children will be on each team? _____.

Problem 2 Mr. Combs is placing 36 players into teams. Each team will have 9 players. How many teams will there be?

Complete the fact family.

$$36 \div 9 = \underline{\hspace{1cm}} \qquad\qquad 36 \div \underline{\hspace{1cm}} = \underline{\hspace{1cm}}$$

$$9 \times \underline{\hspace{1cm}} = 36 \qquad\qquad \underline{\hspace{1cm}} \times 9 = 36$$

Solution How many teams will there be? _____

Apply the GPS

Write a related multiplication and division fact for each array.

1.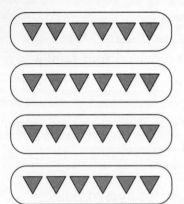

   $24 \div 4 =$ _____

   $4 \times$ _____ $= 24$

2.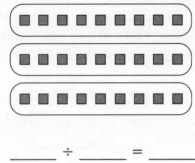

   _____ $\div$ _____ $=$ _____

   _____ $\times$ _____ $=$ _____

3.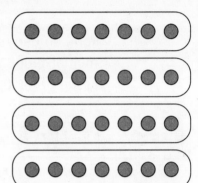

   _____ $\div$ _____ $=$ _____

   _____ $\times$ _____ $=$ _____

Write the related multiplication sentence. Then complete the division fact.

4. $42 \div 7 =$ _____

   $7 \times$ _____ $= 42$

5. $21 \div 3 =$ _____

   _____

6. $72 \div 8 =$ _____

   _____

Complete the fact family.

7. $32 \div 8 = 4$
   $8 \times 4 = 32$
   $4 \times 8 = 32$

   _____

8. $18 \div 6 = 3$
   $3 \times 6 = 18$

   _____

   _____

9. $9 \times 6 = 54$
   $54 \div 6 = 9$

   _____

   _____

Solve each problem. Use related multiplication facts to help, if you wish.

10. Some friends are planting 20 trees in a garden. They want to make 4 rows of trees. They want to plant an equal number of trees in each row. How many trees should they plant in each row? _____

11. Althea says she can use $5 \times 9 = 45$ to check her answer for $45 \div 9$. Is she correct? Explain.

   _____

 Measuring Up® to the Georgia Performance Standards

CRCT Practice Directions: Choose the best answer for each question.
Circle the letter for the answer you have chosen.

1. Mrs. Neal gave 24 pennies to her three children to share equally. How many pennies should each child receive?

   A. 6

   B. 8

   C. 21

   D. 27

2. Which number sentence is related to $56 \div 8 = 7$?

   A. $7 \times 8 = 56$

   B. $56 \div 2 = 28$

   C. $56 \times 7 = 392$

   D. $56 \times 8 = 448$

 3. Which number sentence is NOT related to $72 \div 8 = 9$?

   A. $9 \times 8 = 72$

   B. $72 \div 9 = 8$

   C. $8 \times 9 = 72$

   D. $72 \div 6 = 12$

 4. Jeremy had 63 baseball cards. He gave an equal number of the cards to each of his seven friends. Which of these shows how many cards each friend received?

   A. 63×7

   B. $63 \div 7$

   C. $63 + 7$

   D. $63 - 7$

5. What is the missing number?

	÷ 4
16	4
	7
24	6

   A. 11

   B. 17

   C. 23

   D. 28

Lesson 17 — Divide by 1-Digit Divisors

M4N4.a	Understand the relationship between dividend, divisor, quotient, and remainder.
M4N4.c	Know the division facts with understanding and fluency.
M4N7.d	Use mental math and estimation strategies to compute.
M4P1.b	Solve single and multi-step routine word problems related to all appropriate fourth-grade math standards.

You can use place value, multiplication, and subtraction to help divide.

dividend	the number being divided	$36 \div 9 = 4$
divisor	the number you are dividing by	dividend divisor quotient
quotient	the answer in a division problem	$4 \leftarrow$ quotient divisor $\rightarrow 9\overline{)36} \leftarrow$ dividend

Guided Instruction

Problem

Rita is putting beads into bags. She has 714 beads and wants to put 3 beads into each bag. How many bags of beads can Rita make?

Use the steps of dividing, multiplying, and subtracting to find the quotient.

Step 1   Write the division example.

$3\overline{)714}$

Divide the hundreds. Use mental math, if you can.

How many groups of 3 are in 7? _____

$\begin{array}{r} 2 \\ 3\overline{)714} \\ 6 \end{array}$

Multiply the hundreds quotient by the divisor: $2 \times 3 = 6$

Write the product under the hundreds place.

$\begin{array}{r} 2 \\ 3\overline{)714} \\ -6\downarrow \\ \hline 11 \end{array}$

Subtract and compare: $7 - 6 =$ _____

Then bring down the tens.

Step 2   **Divide** the tens: $11 \div 3 =$ _____

$\begin{array}{r} 23 \\ 3\overline{)714} \\ -6 \\ \hline 11 \\ -\ 9\downarrow \\ \hline 24 \end{array}$

Multiply the tens quotient by the divisor: $3 \times 3 =$ _____

Write and **subtract** the product: $11 - 9 =$ _____

Then bring down the ones.

Step 3   **Divide** the ones: $24 \div 3 =$ _____

$\begin{array}{r} 238 \\ 3\overline{)714} \\ -6 \\ \hline 11 \\ -\ 9 \\ \hline 24 \\ -\ 24 \\ \hline 0 \end{array}$

Multiply the ones quotient by the divisor: $8 \times 3 =$ _____

Write and **subtract** the product: $24 - 24 =$ _____

Compare the result to the divisor: $0 < 3$, so division is complete.

Solution   How many bags can Rita make? _____

Measuring Up® to the Georgia Performance Standards

Apply the GPS

Find the quotient.

1. $51 \div 3 =$ _____

2. $98 \div 7 =$ _____

3. $912 \div 4 =$ _____

4. $896 \div 8 =$ _____

5. $5\overline{)595}$

6. $3\overline{)78}$

7. $6\overline{)732}$

8. $9\overline{)990}$

Complete the statement.

9. $108 \boxed{} 9 = 12$

10. $186 \boxed{} 6 = 31$

11. $18 \boxed{} 7 = 126$

Solve each problem.

12. Cindi was making bags of party favors. She had 96 toys to put in 6 bags. She wanted to put the same number of toys in each bag. How many toys did she put in each bag? _____

13. Shawn says he can use $203 \times 4 = 812$ to check his answer for $812 \div 4$. Can the fact $203 \times 4 = 812$ help you check $812 \div 4$? Explain.

_____

_____

14. Mrs. Cruz drove 123 miles the first week. She drove 134 miles the second week and 127 miles the third week. Suppose Mrs. Cruz drove the same total number of miles and an equal number each week. How many miles would she have driven each week? Explain the operations you used to find out.

_____

_____

CRCT Practice

**Directions: Choose the best answer for each question.
Circle the letter for the answer you have chosen.**

1. Find the quotient.

   $$4\overline{)892}$$

   A. 223
   B. 224
   C. 230
   D. 233

2. Which is NOT a method for checking
   $4 \times 137 = 548$?

   A. $137 \div 4$
   B. $548 \div 4$
   C. $548 \div 137$
   D. $137 + 137 + 137 + 137$

3. Perry has 120 photos. He puts 8 photos on each page of his photo album. How many pages does he fill?

   A. 10
   B. 12
   C. 15
   D. 18

4. Tamara is making baskets of fruit as gifts. She has 78 apples and 6 baskets. She wants to put the same number of apples in each basket. How many apples should she put in each basket?

   A. 72
   B. 26
   C. 16
   D. 13

5. Len read a whole book in 3 weeks. He read 64 pages the first week, 63 pages the second week, and 68 pages the third week. Suppose Len had read an equal number of pages each week. What method should you use to find how many pages he should read each week?

   A. Add the first two numbers, divide by two, and then add the third.

   B. Add all three numbers and divide by three.

   C. Subtract the least number from the greatest number.

   D. Multiply the three numbers and then divide by three.

Lesson 18 Interpret Remainders

M4N4.c   Understand the relationship between dividend, divisor, quotient, and remainder.

M4P1.b   Solve single and multi-step routine word problems related to all appropriate fourth-grade math standards.

M4P2   Students will investigate, develop, and evaluate mathematical arguments.

Sometimes a number cannot be evenly divided. The amount left over is called a **remainder**. The remainder is always less than the divisor.

Guided Instruction

Problem

Ed has 635 T-shirts that he wants to sort into 4 equal groups. How many T-shirts can he put in each group? Will there be any T-shirts left over? If so, how many?

Use steps to find the quotient and any remainder.

Step 1   **Divide** the hundreds.

How many groups of 4 are in 6? _____

Multiply the hundreds quotient by the divisor: $1 \times 4 = 4$

Record the product below.

Subtract: $6 - 4 =$ _____

Then bring down the tens.

$$\begin{array}{r} 1 \\ 4\overline{)635} \\ -4\downarrow \\ \hline 23 \end{array}$$

Step 2   **Divide** the tens: $23 \div 4 =$ _____

Multiply: $5 \times 4 =$ _____

Record the product below.

Subtract: $23 - 20 =$ _____

Then bring down the ones.

$$\begin{array}{r} 15 \\ 4\overline{)635} \\ -4| \\ \hline 23 \\ -20\downarrow \\ \hline 35 \end{array}$$

Step 3   **Divide** the ones: $35 \div 4 =$ _____

Multiply: $8 \times 4 =$ _____

Record the product below.

Subtract: $35 - 32 =$ _____

Compare the result to the divisor. $3 < 4$, so the division is complete.

Record the remainder in the quotient after the letter R.

$$\begin{array}{r} 158 \text{ R3} \\ 4\overline{)635} \\ -4 \\ \hline 23 \\ -20 \\ \hline 35 \\ -32 \\ \hline 3 \end{array}$$

Solution

How many T-shirts can he put in each group? _____

Will there be any left over? _____ If so, how many? _____

Apply the GPS

Divide.

1. 79 ÷ 3 =

_____

2. 97 ÷ 2 =

_____

3. 751 ÷ 4 =

_____

4. 632 ÷ 5 =

_____

5. 4)583

6. 7)95

7. 9)992

8. 8)985

Solve each problem. Explain the operation you used.

9. Nina is making bracelets to give out as gifts. She had 95 charms and 6 bracelets to make. She wants to put the same number of charms on each bracelet. How many charms will she put on each bracelet? _____

Will there be any charms left over? If so, how many? _____

Explain the operation you used to find out. _____

_____

_____

10. The 7 schools in Clark Valley collected 99 books to give to a community center. Each school collected about the same number of books. Estimate the number of books that each school collected. _____

Explain the operation you used and why your estimate is correct. _____

_____

_____

_____

11. Owen wants to put the stones in his collection into boxes. He has 29 blue stones and 38 white stones. He wants to put 5 stones in each box. How many boxes will Owen need so that no stones are left over? _____

Explain the operations you used. _____

_____

_____

Directions: Choose the best answer for each question.
Circle the letter for the answer you have chosen.

1. Find the quotient.

   $$3\overline{)851}$$

   A. 279 R4

   B. 283 R2

   C. 319 R4

   D. 1,183 R2

2. Mr. Block is putting the students into soccer teams. There are 58 students and 4 teams. What would you do to find out how many students he needs to put in each team?

   A. add

   B. subtract

   C. multiply

   D. divide

 3. Which division problem does NOT have a quotient with a remainder?

   A. 678 ÷ 5

   B. 529 ÷ 4

   C. 345 ÷ 3

   D. 296 ÷ 7

4. There are 49 computers to give out to 3 schools in Hart Valley. All the schools will get about the same number of computers. About how many computers will each school get?

   A. 16

   B. 18

   C. 46

   D. 52

 5. Lisa wants to put the stickers in her collection on pages. She has 38 animal stickers and 45 flower stickers. She wants to put 6 stickers on each page. How many pages will Lisa need so that no stickers are left over?

   A. 14

   B. 13

   C. 12

   D. 11

Lesson 19 Divide by 2-Digit Divisors

M4N4.a   Know the division facts with understanding and fluency.
M4N4.b   Solve problems involving division by a 2-digit number (including those that generate a remainder).
M4P1.b   Solve single and multi-step routine word problems related to all appropriate fourth-grade math standards.
M4P4   Students will understand how mathematical ideas interconnect and build on one another and apply mathematics in other content areas.

You can divide by a 2-digit divisor. Use the same steps of division, multiplication, and subtraction to divide as you use with 1-digit divisors. Sometimes there will be a remainder.

Guided Instruction

Problem

Pam is using tiles to make artwork on walls. She has 734 tiles and wants to put the same number of tiles on each of 16 walls. How many tiles should Pam put on each wall? Will there be any tiles left over? How many?

Step 1   **Divide** the hundreds.

Are there any groups of 16 in 7? _____

Use the next place in the dividend.

$$16\overline{)734}$$

Step 2   **Divide** the tens.

How many groups of 16 are in 73? Estimate. _____

Multiply $4 \times$ _____ and record the product below.

Subtract $73 -$ _____ and bring down the ones.

$$\begin{array}{r} 4 \\ 16\overline{)734} \\ -\,64\downarrow \\ \hline 94 \end{array}$$

Step 3   **Divide** the ones.

How many groups of 16 are in 94? Estimate. _____

Multiply _____ $\times\ 16$ and record the product below.

Subtract $94 -$ _____ $=$ _____

Compare the result to the divisor: $14 < 16$, so division is complete.

$$\begin{array}{r} 45 \\ 16\overline{)734} \\ -\,64 \\ \hline 94 \\ -\,80 \\ \hline 14 \end{array}$$

Write the remainder in the quotient.

Why is it possible to have a remainder with 2 digits?

$$\begin{array}{r} 45\ \textbf{R14} \\ 16\overline{)734} \\ -\,64 \\ \hline 94 \\ -\,80 \\ \hline 14 \end{array}$$

_____

_____

Solution

How many tiles should Pam put on each wall? _____

Will there be any tiles left over? _____ How many? _____

Apply the GPS

Divide.

1. $389 \div 14 =$ _____

2. $792 \div 15 =$ _____

3. $595 \div 13 =$ _____

4. $456 \div 17 =$ _____

5. $18\overline{)628}$

6. $12\overline{)119}$

7. $19\overline{)986}$

8. $16\overline{)621}$

Find the missing factor or divisor.

9. $12 \times \boxed{} = 132$ _____

10. $195 \div \boxed{} = 13$ _____

11. $17 \times \boxed{} = 221$ _____

Solve each problem. Explain the operation you used.

12. The climbing school has 358 students. It wants to put the students into equal teams of 15 climbers. How many teams will they make? How many students will be left over? _____

Explain the operation you used to find out. _____

_____

13. Hope School needs to make 618 programs for music night. The 19 classes at the school will each make an equal number of programs. When they are finished, how many programs will still need to be made? _____

Explain the operation you used. _____

_____

_____

14. Amy puts her coins into the pages of an album. She has 156 silver coins and 129 copper coins. She puts 16 coins on each page. How many pages does she need so that no coins are left over? _____

Explain the operations you used. _____

_____

_____

CRCT Practice   **Directions: Choose the best answer for each question.**
Circle the letter for the answer you have chosen.

1. Find the quotient.

$$16\overline{)572}$$

   A   9,152

   B.   36 R0

   C.   35 R12

   D.   35 R2

2. Devon needs to put some rocks into display cases at the museum. There are 169 land rocks and 97 sea rocks. He needs to put 18 rocks into each case. How many cases will Devon need so that no rocks are left over?

   A.   14

   B.   15

   C.   248

   D.   284

3. Which division problem does NOT have a quotient with a remainder?

   A.   756 ÷ 18

   B.   430 ÷ 11

   C.   614 ÷ 24

   D.   385 ÷ 15

4. There are 485 books to give out to 17 classes. All the classes will get the same number of books. How many books will be left over after the books are given out to the classes?

   A.   9

   B.   17

   C.   28

   D.   468

5. What is the missing divisor?

$$195 \div \boxed{} = 13$$

   A.   14

   B.   15

   C.   182

   D.   208

Lesson 20 Patterns in Division

M4N4.a   Know the division facts with understanding and fluency.

M4N4.c   Understand the relationship between dividend, divisor, quotient, and remainder.

M4N4.d   Understand and explain the effect on the quotient of multiplying or dividing both the divisor and dividend by the same number. (2050 ÷ 50 yields the same answer as 205 ÷ 5)

You can use place value, mental math, and patterns to help you divide large numbers. When both the dividend and divisor end in 0, you can divide each by 10 and solve the problem using smaller numbers.

Guided Instruction

Problem

There are 3,050 seats at the town baseball field. Each section has the same number of seats. There are 50 sections. How many seats are in each section?

Step 1   Write the division problem.

Both numbers end in 0, so you can divide each number by 10.

3,050 ÷ 10 = _____

50 ÷ 10 = _____

$3{,}050 \div 50 = ?$

Step 2   Divide using the smaller numbers.
Use mental math, if you can.

```
    61
5)305
  -30↓
    05
   - 5
     0
```

Step 3   Use multiplication to check that the quotient is correct for the actual numbers in the problem.

Check:
```
    61
  × 50
 3,050
```

Solution   How many seats are in each section? _____

Other Examples

40 ÷ 20 = 2	60 ÷ 20 = 3	90 ÷ 30 = 3	80 ÷ 40 = _____
400 ÷ 20 = 20	600 ÷ 20 = 30	900 ÷ 30 = 30	800 ÷ 40 = _____
4,000 ÷ 20 = 200	6,000 ÷ 20 = 300	9,000 ÷ 30 = 300	8,000 ÷ 40 = _____

Apply the GPS

Write the numbers to complete each pattern.

1. $2{,}170 \div 70 = 31$

$217 \div \underline{\hspace{1cm}} = 31$

2. $1{,}460 \div 20 = 73$

$\underline{\hspace{1cm}} \div 2 = 73$

3. $4{,}080 \div 80 = 51$

$\underline{\hspace{1cm}} \div 8 = 51$

4. $60 \div 30 = 2$

$600 \div 30 = 20$

$6{,}000 \div 30 = \underline{\hspace{1cm}}$

5. $50 \div 10 = 5$

$500 \div 10 = 50$

$5{,}000 \div 10 = \underline{\hspace{1cm}}$

6. $80 \div 20 = 4$

$800 \div 20 = 40$

$\underline{\hspace{1cm}} \div 20 = 400$

Find the quotient. Use smaller numbers and mental math, if you wish. You can multiply to check your answer.

7. $50\overline{)2{,}550}$

8. $60\overline{)4{,}260}$

9. $30\overline{)9{,}060}$

10. $40\overline{)2{,}800}$

Solve each problem. Use smaller numbers and mental math, if you wish.

11. This summer, 1,360 people attended the Buena City soccer matches. This fall, 2,000 people attended. The same number of people attended each of the 30 matches held this year. How many people attended each match? _____

12. Amir put snack packages of cookies into cartons to ship. There are 1,060 snack packages and 20 cartons. He put the same number of snack packages in each carton. How many snack packages did he put in each carton?

_____

13. Mr. Han drives 40 miles each day for work. He drove 4,000 miles in the first half of the year and 4,400 miles in the second half of the year. How many days has he driven the truck this year? _____

Explain the operations that you used. _____

_____

_____

_____

   Measuring Up® to the Georgia Performance Standards

Directions: Choose the best answer for each question.
Circle the letter for the answer you have chosen.

1. Find the quotient.

$$30 \overline{)9,030}$$

A. 101

B. 201

C. 301

D. 302

2. Mrs. Tam is giving out drawing paper to the art students. She has 1,750 sheets of paper and 50 art students. She wants to give the same number of sheets to each student. How many sheets should each student get?

A. 32

B. 35

C. 150

D. 350

3. Which has the same answer as $1,240 \div 40$?

A. $40 \times 1,240$

B. $124 \div 4$

C. $124 \div 40$

D. $1,240 \div 31$

4. Nilda has to read three books that have a total of 2,840 pages. She has 20 days to read the pages. She wants to read the same number of pages each day. Which is the BEST method for finding out how many pages she should read each day?

A. divide 2,840 by 2

B. divide 284 by 2

C. multiply 284 by 20

D. subtract 20 from 2,840 and then divide by 20

5. Solve the problem:

$$2,520 \div 40 = ?$$

A. 63

B. 65

C. 630

D. 605

Lesson 21 Estimate Quotients

M4N4.d	Understand and explain the effect on the quotient of multiplying or dividing both the divisor and dividend by the same number. (2050 ÷ 50 yields the same answer as 205 ÷ 5)
M4N7.d	Use mental math and estimation strategies to compute.
M4P1.b	Solve single and multi-step routine word problems related to all appropriate fourth-grade math standards.
M4P1.c	Determine the operation(s) needed to solve a problem.

You can use compatible numbers when an exact quotient is not needed.
Compatible numbers are close to the actual numbers and divide easily.
Sometimes you can round numbers to make them compatible.

Guided Instruction

Problem 1

The Carl School computer room has 62 computers. There are 7 classes in the fourth grade. Each fourth-grade class uses about the same number of computers at computer time. About how many computers does each class get?

Use compatible numbers for the dividend and divisor.

Step 1 The problem asks for **about** how many, so you can estimate.

Think of a division fact that is close.

62 ÷ 7 is close to ⟶ 63 ÷ 7

Step 2 Use mental math to divide with the compatible numbers.

63 ÷ 7 = _____

Solution About how many computers does each class get? about _____

Guided Instruction

Problem 2

The Daly School is giving away books to 40 libraries. The school has 2,789 books to give away. If each library gets about the same number of books, about how many books does each library get?

Step 1 Use compatible numbers and a division fact that is close.

Think: 2,789 ÷ 40 is close to ⟶ 2,800 ÷ 40

2,800 is 2,789 rounded to the nearest hundred.

Step 2 Use mental math to divide with the compatible numbers.

Think: 2,800 ÷ 40   Use smaller numbers.

↓   ↓

280 ÷ 4 = _____

Solution About how many books does each library get? about _____

 Measuring Up® to the Georgia Performance Standards

Apply the GPS

Estimate each quotient. Use compatible numbers.

1. 47 ÷ 9 =

about _____

2. 554 ÷ 80 =

about _____

3. 3,129 ÷ 60 =

about _____

4. 7)43

about _____

5. 6)538

about _____

6. 2,473 ÷ 50 =

about _____

7. 8)4,761

about _____

8. 132 ÷ 4=

about _____

Estimate to answer each problem. Use compatible numbers.

9. There are 49 plants that need to be planted at the town park. There are 6 areas in the park. All the areas will have about the same number of plants. About how many plants will there be in each area? _____

10. Mrs. Lam has 58 apples to give out to the campers. There are 8 camping groups on the trip. If all the groups get about the same number of apples, about how many apples does each group get? _____

Use the table to solve problems 11–13. Use compatible numbers.

11. Sula has $25. Jon has $19. What is the greatest number of long-sleeve shirts they can buy together?

_____

12. Mark has $32. He needs to buy one jacket and some T-shirts. What is the greatest number of T-shirts he can buy? _____

13. Mrs. Cole bought some skirts. The total cost was $45, including tax. How many skirts did she most likely buy?

_____

Explain how you found your answer.

_____

_____

_____

Wee-Town Children's Clothing Shop

Item	Cost
T-shirts	$4
Shorts or Skirts	$7
Long-sleeve Shirts	$6
Jacket	$9

Directions: Choose the best answer for each question. Circle the letter for the answer you have chosen.

1. There are 73 playgrounds in Kalb County. There are 8 towns in the county. If all the towns have about the same number of playgrounds, about how many playgrounds are there in each town?

   A. 8

   B. 9

   C. 65

   D. 81

 2. The table below shows Joe's driving log.

Week	Miles Driven	Hours Driven
1	3,050	50
2	3,600	40

   Which can be used to find how many miles Joe drove each hour in Week 1?

   A. 305 ÷ 5

   B. 350 ÷ 5

   C. 3,600 ÷ 4

   D. 3,600 × 40

3. Which is the BEST etsimate:

   $$725 ÷ 8 = ?$$

   A. 70

   B. 80

   C. 90

   D. 100

 4. The table below shows the hours worked and the pay for two workers.

Name	Number of Hours Worked	Total Pay
Colby	30	$221
Katie	40	$355

   Which is the BEST estimate of how much more Katie makes each hour than Colby?

   A. $1

   B. $5

   C. $8

   D. $9

5. Workers at Rose Community Center were building walls around some gardens. They had 1,514 building bricks to start. Then 2,000 more bricks arrived. The bricks were used equally on six walls. Which shows one way to find about how many bricks were used on each wall?

   A. 3,500 − 6

   B. 6 × 3,600

   C. 3,600 ÷ 6

   D. 3,500 ÷ 5

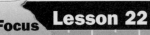

Focus on GPS

Lesson 22 Problem-Solving Strategy: Determine the Operation

M4N7.a	Describe situations in which the four operations may be used and the relationships among them.
M4N7.b	Compute using the order of operations, including parentheses.
M4N7.c	Compute using the commutative, associative, and distributive properties.
M4P1.b	Solve single and multi-step routine word problems related to all appropriate fourth-grade math standards.
M4P1.c	Determine the operation(s) needed to solve a problem.

You can decide which operations can help to solve problems.

Addition	If you are putting parts together, you can add.
Subtraction	If you are separating a part from a whole, you can subtract.
Multiplication	If you are putting equal parts together, you can multiply.
Division	If you are separating a whole into equal parts, you can divide.

Guided Instruction

Problem

Alan's sports club is having a team race day. There are 6 teams, with 4 swimmers and 3 runners on each team. How many team members are there in all?

Find if adding, subtracting, multiplying, or dividing helps solve the problem.

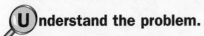

Understand the problem.

You need to find _____.

There are 4 swimmers and 3 runners on each team.

To put the parts together, you can _____.

You know that the 6 teams are equal.

To put together equal groups, you can _____.

Make a plan.

You can write a number sentence.

$6 \times (4 + 3)$ ◄—— The parentheses ( ) show which operation you should do first.

Solve the problem.

Solve the number sentence. $6 \times (4 + 3)$
                                              ↓
                                $6 \times \quad 7 =$ _____

How many team members are there in all? _____

Check your answer.

What is another method to solve? Explain it and use it to check.

_____

_____

Apply the GPS

Solve each problem. Write the operation(s) you used.

1. Manny earned $8 each hour. He worked 4 hours each day for two days. Then he worked 2 hours on the third day. How much money did he earn in all in the three days?

_____

_____

2. There were 5 large plates and 3 small plates. Hal needs to put the same number of tomatoes on each plate. He has 24 tomatoes in all. How many tomatoes should he put on each plate?

_____

_____

3. Jana collected 156 leaves. She kept 36 of the leaves and gave the rest to her friends. She gave 15 leaves to each friend. How many friends did she give leaves to?

_____

_____

4. A book has four chapters and 312 pages in all. Chapter 1 has 64 pages. Chapter 2 has 87 pages. Chapter 3 has 109 pages. How many pages does Chapter 4 have?

_____

_____

Solve each problem. Choose an operation and explain your method.

5. A farmer's land can hold 132 plants. The farmer wants at least 10 plants in each row and at least 10 rows. How should the farmer arrange the plants so that they are in equal rows? Include how many plants should be in each row and the number of rows. Explain your method.

_____

_____

_____

6. Tamela is making fruit punch for a party. She started with an empty bowl. She poured in 4 cups of grape juice, 3 cups of apple juice, 6 cups of cranberry juice, and 5 cups of orange juice. Then she poured half of the punch from the bowl into a pitcher. How many cups of punch were left in the bowl? Explain your method.

_____

_____

CRCT Practice

Directions: Choose the best answer for each question. Circle the letter for the answer you have chosen.

1. A group of 362 students chose which day is their favorite. Their choices were Friday, Saturday, or Sunday. 94 students chose Friday. 179 students chose Saturday. How many students chose Sunday?

   A. 635
   B. 273
   C. 247
   D. 89

2. Charlie has 91 stickers. He wants to put all the stickers on one page of his sticker book. How should Charlie arrange the stickers so that they are in equal rows?

   A. 9 rows of 10
   B. 7 rows of 13
   C. 9 rows of 9
   D. 8 rows of 11

3. The students voted on the color for their sports uniforms. Their choices were blue, purple, or red. There were 412 students. 180 students chose blue. 79 students chose purple. How many students chose red?

   A. 137
   B. 153
   C. 162
   D. 232

4. Aliya put together lunch bags to give out at a class trip. She had 92 napkins to put in 23 bags. She put an equal number of napkins in each bag. What would you do to find out how many napkins she put in each bag?

   A. add
   B. subtract
   C. multiply
   D. divide

5. The book club is having a book sale. There are 4 tables, with 7 picture books and 5 chapter books on each table. How many books are there in all?

   A. 16
   B. 39
   C. 48
   D. 140

Directions: Choose the best answer for each question.
Circle the letter for the answer you have chosen.

1. Which number sentence correctly represents this picture?

   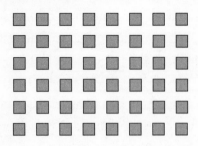

   A. $6 + 6 + 6 + 6 + 6 + 6 = 36$

   B. $6 + 8 = 14$

   C. $6 \times 8 = 48$

   D. $8 \times 8 = 64$

2. Find the quotient.

   $$50\overline{)1{,}050}$$

   A. 21

   B. 25

   C. 201

   D. 210

3. Which symbol belongs in the ☐ ?

   $153 \boxed{} 9 = 17$

   A. $+$

   B. $-$

   C. $\times$

   D. $\div$

 4. Ming Hwa has 80 animal stamps and 37 flower stamps. She wants to put all the stamps on one page of her sticker book. How should she arrange the stamps so that they are in equal rows?

   A. 8 rows of 14

   B. 10 rows of 8

   C. 12 rows of 8

   D. 13 rows of 9

5. There are 228 students who will sit in the cafeteria. Each table can fit 14 students. How many tables will be needed so that every student can sit?

   A. 16

   B. 17

   C. 21

   D. 242

6. The table below shows the amounts Harry and Nola earned for doing chores.

Name	Number of Days Worked	Total Amount
Harry	20	$83
Nola	30	$152

Which is the BEST estimate of how much Harry made each day doing chores?

A. $2

B. $4

C. $20

D. $40

 7. The Everson School received some deliveries of school supplies. First 1,375 pencils arrived. Then 1,725 more pencils arrived. If the pencils were given out equally to 50 classes, about how many pencils did each class get?

A. 3,150

B. 600

C. 60

D. 50

8. Which has the same answer as 6,040 ÷ 20?

A. 20 × 6,040

B. 6,040 ÷ 2

C. 640 ÷ 2

D. 604 ÷ 2

9. Pearl saved $7 each week for 6 weeks. Then she spent $6 on a book. She used what was left for gifts for 4 family members. She spent an equal amount on each family member. How much did Pearl spend on each family member?

A. $32

B. $23

C. $12

D. $9

10. Jocelyn had 34 picture frames. Then she got 6 more picture frames. She put 5 picture frames into each box. How many boxes did Jocelyn need for all the picture frames?

A. 5

B. 8

C. 35

D. 45

11. At the state sports games, there are 327 students playing softball and 514 students playing soccer. There are 15 schools at the games. If all the schools have about the same number of students playing, about how many students are there from each school?

    A. 56

    B. 63

    C. 416

    D. 826

12. Find the quotient.

    $$4\overline{)95}$$

    A. 23 R3

    B. 23 R4

    C. 380

    D. 113 R3

13. In the following story problem, select the BEST method for solving it:

    > Luis visited his aunt who lives in River Falls. He brought back 472 stones and gave 8 stones to each friend. How many friends received stones from Luis?

    A. add

    B. subtract

    C. multiply

    D. divide

14. Janet is setting the tables for a party. There are 3 tables, with 5 large plates and 4 small plates on each table. How many plates are there in all?

    A. 9

    B. 12

    C. 27

    D. 60

15. At the holiday picnic, first 75 people arrived. Then 87 more people arrived. They sat at 9 long tables with an equal number of people at each table. How many people sat at each table?

    A. 18

    B. 19

    C. 153

    D. 162

16. What is the missing divisor?

    $$132 \div \boxed{} = 12$$

    A. 11

    B. 12

    C. 120

    D. 144

17. Barry wants to paste his collection of bug pictures onto pages. He has 173 pictures of flying bugs and 129 pictures of crawling bugs. He wants to put 4 pictures on each page. How many pages will Barry need so that no pictures are left over?

A. 11

B. 75

C. 76

D. 298

18. Complete the fact family.

$9 \times 8 = 72$, $8 \times 9 = 72$,

$72 \div 9 = 8$, _____

A. $72 - 8 = 64$

B. $72 \div 6 = 12$

C. $72 \div 8 = 9$

D. $72 \times 9 = 648$

19. There are 50 students who want to be in hobby groups. There are 6 hobby groups. If all the hobby groups have about the same number of students, about how many students are there in each group?

A. 6

B. 7

C. 8

D. 56

20. Mr. Sands delivered 3,960 packs of paper to 30 stores. Each store got the same number of packs. How many packs of paper did each store get?

A. 132

B. 1,320

C. 3,930

D. 3,990

21. Tamiya put the buttons in her collection into bags. She had 581 buttons. She put the same number of buttons into each of 6 bags. How many buttons were left over after Tamiya finished?

A. 5

B. 11

C. 96

D. 576

M4N6	Students will further develop their understanding of the meaning of common fractions.
M4N6.c	Convert and use mixed numbers and improper fractions interchangeably.
M4P1.b	Solve single and multi-step routine word problems related to all appropriate fourth-grade math standards.
M4P5	Students will create and use pictures, manipulatives, models, and symbols to organize, record, and communicate mathematical ideas.

You can use a **fraction** to name a part of a whole or part of a group. The **numerator** shows how many parts you are counting. The **denominator** shows the total number of equal parts in the whole or group.

$$\frac{3}{4} \leftarrow \text{numerator} \rightarrow \frac{3}{4}$$
$$\quad\leftarrow \text{denominator} \rightarrow$$

A fraction that shows an amount less than 1 is a **proper fraction**. An **improper fraction** names an amount equal to or greater than 1. It has a numerator that is equal to or greater than the denominator. A **mixed number** names an amount greater than 1. It has a whole number and a fraction.

mixed number $1\frac{1}{2}$ $\frac{3}{2}$ improper fraction

Guided Instruction

Problem 1

A class of ten students is planning a party. Four of the students promise to bring food to the party. What fraction of the class will bring food?

Use a model to write the fraction.

Step 1   Look at the model above. The students bringing food are circled.

How many students are bringing food? _____

How many students are there in all? _____

Step 2   Write the number of students bringing food as the numerator. Then write the total number of students as the denominator.

___ ⟵ numerator
___ ⟵ denominator

Step 3   Write the word name of the fraction. We read $\frac{4}{10}$ as "four-tenths."

Solution   What fraction of the class will bring food? _____

Guided Instruction

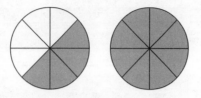
Trina bought two cakes for her party. She cut each cake into 8 equal slices. The guests ate 12 slices of cake. What improper fraction and mixed number name the amount of cake that the guests ate?

Use a model to write the improper fraction and mixed number.

Step 1   Shade the model to show the number of cake slices the guests ate.

Step 2   How many equal parts are shaded? _____

How many parts are in each circle? _____

Write the improper fraction. Write the number of shaded parts over the number of parts in each circle. _____

Step 3   How many whole circles are shaded? _____

What fraction of the second circle is shaded? _____

Write a mixed number for the same amount. Write the whole number and then the fraction. _____

Solution   What improper fraction and mixed number name the amount of cake that the guests ate? _____

Other Examples

Sam needs a piece of wood that is three-fourths of a foot long. What letter on the number line shows three-fourths of a foot?

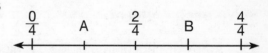

The number line shows one foot that is divided into four equal parts, or fourths. Starting from the left, count off three fourths.

The letter _____ on the number line shows a length of $\frac{3}{4}$ foot.

Sam also needs a piece of wood that is $2\frac{1}{2}$ feet long.

What improper fraction names the same amount as $2\frac{1}{2}$? _____

What fraction names each section of the number line? _____

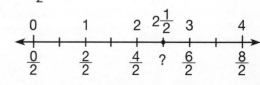

Apply the GPS Write the fraction for each shaded part. Then write the word name for the fraction.

1.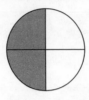

_____

2.

_____

3.

_____

4.

_____

5.

_____

6.

_____

Write the improper fraction and the mixed number for each model.

7.

_____

8.

_____

9.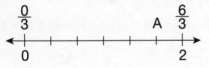

$\frac{0}{3}$ A $\frac{6}{3}$

0   2

_____

10.

$\frac{0}{4}$ B $\frac{8}{4}$

0   2

_____

Solve each problem.

11. A box of chocolates holds 12 pieces of chocolate. Karen gave $\frac{2}{12}$ of the box to her best friend. Then she gave $\frac{5}{12}$ of the box to her teacher. What fraction of the box of chocolates is left? _____

12. How many pieces of this model should be shaded to show $1\frac{3}{6}$?

_____

CRCT Practice

Directions: Choose the best answer for each question.

Circle the letter for the answer you have chosen.

 1. What fraction names the part that is NOT shaded?

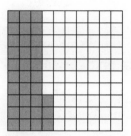

A. $\frac{3}{10}$

B. $\frac{7}{10}$

C. $\frac{33}{100}$

D. $\frac{67}{100}$

 2. Two pies are each cut into 10 slices. One whole pie and six slices of the second pie are eaten. What fraction of the pies is left?

A. $1\frac{6}{10}$

B. $1\frac{10}{6}$

C. $\frac{4}{10}$

D. $\frac{10}{4}$

3. Which number line shows the fraction $\frac{4}{6}$?

A.

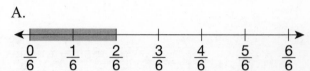

B.

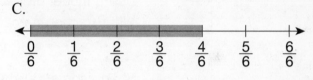

C.

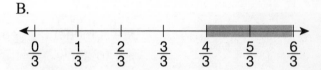

D.

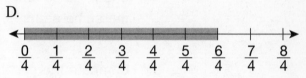

4. A flock of ducks is made up of 10 white ducks and 15 brown ducks. Which fraction describes the part of the flock made up by white ducks?

A. $\frac{10}{15}$

B. $\frac{15}{10}$

C. $\frac{15}{25}$

D. $\frac{10}{25}$

Lesson 24 Find Equivalent Fractions

M4N6.a	Understand representations of simple equivalent fractions.
M4P1.b	Solve single and multi-step routine word problems related to all appropriate fourth-grade math standards.
M4P5	Students will create and use pictures, manipulatives, models, and symbols to organize, record, and communicate mathematical ideas.

You can use models to help you find equivalent fractions. **Equivalent fractions** are two or more fractions that have the same value. They use different numerators and denominators to name the same amount of a whole or of a group.

Guided Instruction

Problem Samantha ate $\frac{1}{2}$ of her hamburger at dinner. What is another fraction that tells how much of the hamburger she ate?

Step 1 Use a model divided into halves. Shade one half to show $\frac{1}{2}$ of the hamburger.

Step 2 Use a model divided into twice as many parts. What fraction names each part?

_____

Shade some fourths until the shaded area is the same as for $\frac{1}{2}$.

Step 3 Compare the parts that are shaded.

How many fourths are shaded? _____

Write the equivalent fraction: $\frac{1}{2} =$ _____

Solution What is another fraction that names $\frac{1}{2}$? _____

Another Example

What are two fractions that are equal to $\frac{1}{4}$?

Shade $\frac{1}{4}$ of the model.

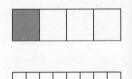

Shade the same area on this model.
What fraction does the shaded part show? _____

Shade the same area on this model.
What fraction does the shaded part show? _____

Write the equivalent fractions: $\frac{1}{4} =$ _____ $=$ _____

       Measuring Up® to the Georgia Performance Standards

Apply the GPS

Color the models to show equivalent fractions. Then write the equivalent fractions.

1.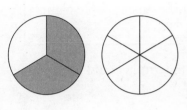

_____ = _____

2.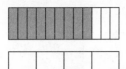

_____ = _____

3.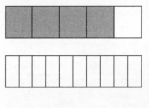

_____ = _____

4.

_____ = _____

5.

_____ = _____

6.

_____ = _____

Decide whether the fractions in each pair are equivalent. Write *yes* or *no*. Use the fraction strips to the right to help you.

7. $\frac{1}{2}$ and $\frac{3}{6}$

_____

8. $\frac{3}{4}$ and $\frac{2}{3}$

_____

9. 1 and $\frac{6}{6}$

_____

10. $\frac{8}{10}$ and $\frac{10}{12}$

_____

11. $\frac{3}{5}$ and $\frac{2}{4}$

_____

12. $\frac{1}{3}$ and $\frac{4}{12}$

_____

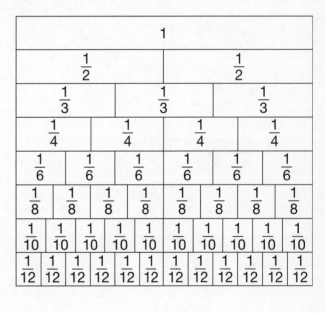

Solve each problem.

13. Emily fills a four-cup pitcher with three cups of water. What is the equivalent fraction for a pitcher that holds twelve cups? _____

14. What is an equivalent fraction for the two-twelfths shown in the model?

Explain. _____

_____

CRCT Practice

Directions: Choose the best answer for each question.

Circle the letter for the answer you have chosen.

1. Which fraction is NOT the same as

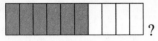 ?

    A. $\dfrac{18}{30}$

    B. $\dfrac{12}{20}$

    C. $\dfrac{3}{5}$

    D. $\dfrac{1}{2}$

2. Which model shows an equivalent fraction to $\dfrac{1}{3}$?

    A.

    B.

    C.

    D.

Use the information in the box below to answer questions 3 and 4.

> Ramon invited a group of 12 people to his party. Two of the people he invited were busy and could not come. All of the other people came to the party.

3. What part of the group could NOT come to Ramon's party?

    A. $\dfrac{2}{8}$

    B. $\dfrac{4}{8}$

    C. $\dfrac{1}{6}$

    D. $\dfrac{4}{6}$

4. Which fraction is the same as the part of the group that did come to the party?

    A. $\dfrac{1}{4}$

    B. $\dfrac{5}{6}$

    C. $\dfrac{7}{8}$

    D. $\dfrac{9}{10}$

Lesson 25 Add Fractions

M4N6.b Add and subtract fractions and mixed numbers with common denominators.

M4P1.b Solve single and multi-step routine word problems related to all appropriate fourth-grade math standards.

M4P5 Students will create and use pictures, manipulatives, models, and symbols to organize, record, and communicate mathematical ideas.

You can use models to add fractions with common denominators. You can also add fractions with common denominators by adding the numerators. The denominator stays the same.

Guided Instruction

Problem Sarah and James are working on a jigsaw puzzle. Sarah has finished $\frac{2}{10}$ of the puzzle. James has finished $\frac{5}{10}$. How much of the puzzle have they finished altogether?

Use a model to help you add $\frac{2}{10}$ and $\frac{5}{10}$.

Step 1 Use a model divided into 10 equal parts or tenths. Shade 2 parts and then 5 parts to show the tenths you are adding.

Step 2 The fractions $\frac{2}{10}$ and $\frac{5}{10}$ have the same denominator.

$$\frac{2}{10} + \frac{5}{10} \quad \begin{matrix} \leftarrow \text{numerators} \\ \leftarrow \text{denominators} \end{matrix}$$

To count the total number of shaded parts, add the numerators.

$$2 + 5 = \underline{\qquad}$$

Step 3 Write the sum of the numerators over 10, the common denominator.

$$\frac{2}{10} + \frac{5}{10} = \frac{2+5}{10} = \frac{\boxed{}}{\boxed{}}$$

Solution How much of the puzzle have they finished altogether? _____

Another Example

Amit cut a cake into six pieces. He ate one-sixth of the cake. His brother ate two-sixths of the cake and his sister ate one-sixth. How much of the cake did they eat altogether?

Write the addition problem. _____

The denominators are the same, so add the numerators. Write the sum over the common denominator.

$$\frac{1}{6} + \frac{2}{6} + \frac{1}{6} = \frac{1+2+1}{6} = \frac{\boxed{}}{\boxed{}}$$

Apply the GPS

Add. Use the models to help you find each sum.

1.

   $\frac{2}{4} + \frac{1}{4} =$ _____

2.

   $\frac{1}{6} + \frac{4}{6} =$ _____

3.

   $\frac{1}{3} + \frac{1}{3} + \frac{1}{3} =$ _____

Add. Use models if you want to.

4. $\frac{4}{6} + \frac{1}{6} =$ _____

5. $\frac{5}{8} + \frac{1}{8} =$ _____

6. $\frac{2}{5} + \frac{2}{5} =$ _____

7. $\frac{3}{10} + \frac{5}{10} =$ _____

8. $\frac{6}{12} + \frac{3}{12} =$ _____

9. $\frac{1}{2} + \frac{1}{2} =$ _____

10. $\frac{1}{9} + \frac{3}{9} + \frac{2}{9} =$ _____

11. $\frac{4}{12} + \frac{1}{12} + \frac{3}{12} + \frac{2}{12} =$ _____

Add. Write the word names for each sum.

12. $\frac{2}{8} + \frac{1}{8} + \frac{3}{8} =$ _____

13. $\frac{1}{10} + \frac{2}{10} + \frac{2}{10} + \frac{4}{10} =$ _____

14. three-sixths plus one-sixth equals _____

15. seven-twelfths plus two-twelfths equals _____

Solve each problem.

16. Troy has two opened boxes of cereal. There is some cereal left in each box. Use the models to write a number sentence that shows how much cereal is left altogether.

    _____

    What is the total amount of cereal left? _____

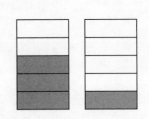

17. The instruments in a school band are $\frac{2}{10}$ drums, $\frac{4}{10}$ brass horns, and $\frac{4}{10}$ other wind instruments. What fraction of the band is made up of drums and brass horns?

    _____

Measuring Up® to the Georgia Performance Standards

CRCT Practice   **Directions: Choose the best answer for each question.**
Circle the letter for the answer you have chosen.

1. Which sum does this model show?

A. $\frac{1}{6} + \frac{1}{6} + \frac{3}{6}$

B. $\frac{1}{6} + \frac{1}{6} + \frac{2}{6}$

C. $\frac{2}{6} + \frac{1}{6} + \frac{2}{6}$

D. $\frac{3}{6} + \frac{1}{6} + \frac{2}{6}$

2. Use the model to find which fraction goes in the box to make the number sentence true.

$\frac{1}{8} + \frac{5}{8} + \frac{1}{8} = \boxed{}$

A. $\frac{7}{8}$

B. $\frac{6}{8}$

C. $\frac{5}{8}$

D. $\frac{5}{8}$

 3. What is the sum of one-twelfth, six-twelfths, and three-twelfths?

A. $\frac{4}{12}$

B. $\frac{7}{12}$

C. $\frac{9}{12}$

D. $\frac{10}{12}$

 4. At a restaurant, $\frac{1}{4}$ of the meals come with a vegetable, $\frac{2}{4}$ of the meals come with a salad, and $\frac{1}{4}$ of the meals come with dessert. What fraction of the meals do NOT come with dessert?

A. $\frac{1}{4}$

B. $\frac{2}{4}$

C. $\frac{3}{4}$

D. $\frac{4}{4}$

Lesson 26 Subtract Fractions

M4N6.b   Add and subtract fractions and mixed numbers with common denominators.
M4P1.b   Solve single and multi-step routine word problems related to all appropriate fourth-grade math standards.
M4P5   Students will create and use pictures, manipulatives, models, and symbols to organize, record, and communicate mathematical ideas.

You can use models to subtract fractions with common denominators. You can also subtract fractions with common denominators by subtracting the numerators. The denominator stays the same.

Guided Instruction

Problem 1 A recipe for chili calls for $\frac{3}{4}$ cup of black beans and $\frac{1}{4}$ cup of onions. How much more beans are in the chili than onions?

Step 1 Use a model divided into 4 equal parts or fourths. Shade 3 fourths to show the amount of black beans.

Step 2 Cross out 1 shaded part to subtract $\frac{1}{4}$ from $\frac{3}{4}$. Count: how many shaded parts are left?

$3 - 1 =$ _____

$\frac{3}{4} - \frac{1}{4}$

Step 3 Write the number of shaded parts left over 4, the common denominator. $\frac{3}{4} - \frac{1}{4} = \dfrac{\boxed{}}{4}$

Solution How much more beans are in the chili? _____ cup

Guided Instruction

Problem 2 Scott lives seven-eighths of a mile from school. He walked one-eighth of a mile and stopped at a stoplight. Then he walked another three-eighths of a mile. How much farther does Scott have to walk?

Step 1 Write the subtraction problem. _____

Step 2 The denominators are the same, so you can subtract the numerators. $7 - 1 - 3 =$ _____

Step 3 Write the difference over the common denominator.

$$\frac{7}{8} - \frac{1}{8} - \frac{3}{8} = \frac{7 - 1 - 3}{8} = \frac{\boxed{}}{\boxed{}}$$

Solution How much farther does Scott have to walk? _____

Apply the GPS

Subtract. Use the models to help you find each difference.

1.

$\frac{4}{5} - \frac{3}{5} =$ _____

2.

$\frac{8}{9} - \frac{4}{9} =$ _____

3.

$\frac{9}{10} - \frac{2}{10} - \frac{1}{10} =$ _____

Subtract. Use models if you want to.

4. $\frac{5}{6} - \frac{3}{6} =$ _____

5. $\frac{3}{5} - \frac{2}{5} =$ _____

6. $\frac{6}{8} - \frac{1}{8} =$ _____

7. $\frac{4}{4} - \frac{3}{4} =$ _____

8. $\frac{11}{12} - \frac{9}{12} =$ _____

9. $\frac{8}{10} - \frac{3}{10} =$ _____

10. $\frac{3}{3} - \frac{1}{3} - \frac{1}{3} =$ _____

11. $\frac{7}{10} - \frac{1}{10} - \frac{3}{10} =$ _____

Write the word name for each difference.

12. $\frac{8}{8} - \frac{1}{8} - \frac{5}{8} =$ _____

13. $\frac{7}{12} - \frac{2}{12} =$ _____

14. six-sevenths minus three-sevenths = _____

15. four-sixths minus one-sixth minus two-sixths = _____

Solve each problem.

16. A soda bottle is filled with $\frac{10}{10}$ liter or one liter of soda. Andy pours $\frac{2}{10}$ liter into one glass and $\frac{3}{10}$ liter into another glass. How much soda is left in the bottle?

_____ liter

17. Marissa buys a box of 12 doughnuts. Half of the doughnuts in the box are chocolate. Marissa eats two of the chocolate doughnuts. What fraction of the box does she have left? Explain your answer.

_____

_____

CRCT Practice

Directions: Choose the best answer for each question.

Circle the letter for the answer you have chosen.

 1. What is the difference of seven-eighths and four-eighths?

A. $\frac{3}{0}$

B. $\frac{3}{3}$

C. $\frac{3}{8}$

D. $\frac{4}{8}$

2. Use the model to subtract:

$$\frac{8}{12} - \frac{3}{12} = ?$$

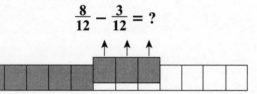

A. $\frac{3}{4}$

B. $\frac{3}{12}$

C. $\frac{5}{0}$

D. $\frac{5}{12}$

3. Subtract:

$$\frac{9}{6} - \frac{2}{6} - \frac{3}{6} = ?$$

A. four-sixths

B. five-sixths

C. six-sixths

D. seven-sixths

 4. At the grocery store, Sara buys $\frac{10}{12}$ pound of walnuts. She will use $\frac{4}{12}$ pound to make brownies and $\frac{5}{12}$ pound to make banana bread. What fraction of the walnuts will NOT be used?

A. $\frac{5}{12}$

B. $\frac{4}{12}$

C. $\frac{1}{12}$

D. $\frac{0}{12}$

Lesson 27 Add Mixed Numbers

M4N6.b Add and subtract fractions and mixed numbers with common denominators.
M4N6.c Convert and use mixed numbers and improper fractions interchangeably.
M4P5 Students will create and use pictures, manipulatives, models, and symbols to organize, record, and communicate mathematical ideas.

You can use models to add mixed numbers with common denominators. You can also add mixed numbers by adding the whole amounts and then adding the fractions. If the sum of the fractions is an improper fraction, change it to a mixed number. Then add the mixed number to the whole number sum.

Guided Instruction

Problem Victor spent $2\frac{2}{4}$ hours on homework and $1\frac{1}{4}$ hours on band practice. How many hours did Victor spend altogether?

Step 1 Shade a model to show $2\frac{2}{4}$ and $1\frac{1}{4}$.

What does each whole strip stand for? _____

What fraction does each part stand for? _____

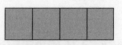

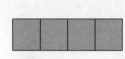
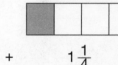
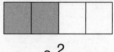

$2\frac{2}{4}$ + $1\frac{1}{4}$

Step 2 Circle the shaded whole strips to combine them.
How many whole strips are shaded? 2 + 1 = _____

Step 3 Circle the extra shaded parts to combine them.
How many extra fourths are shaded? $\frac{2}{4} + \frac{1}{4}$ = _____

Step 4 Write a mixed number to show the total. _____

Solution How many hours did Victor spend altogether? _____

Another Example

Add one and two-thirds and one and two-thirds.

Add the whole amounts. 1 + 1 = _____

Add the fractions. $\frac{2}{3} + \frac{2}{3} = \frac{2+2}{3}$ = _____

$1\frac{2}{3}$ + $1\frac{2}{3}$

Write a mixed number: $2\frac{4}{3}$

Change the improper fraction $\frac{4}{3}$ to a mixed number. $\frac{4}{3}$ = _____

Now add the mixed number to 2 to get the final sum.

$1\frac{2}{3} + 1\frac{2}{3} = 2 + 1\frac{1}{3}$ = _____

Apply the GPS

Use the models to add. Write each sum as a mixed number and improper fraction.

1.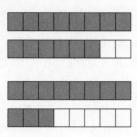

_____

2.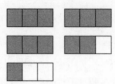

_____

3.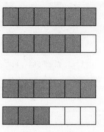

_____

Add. Write each sum as a mixed number and improper fraction.

4. $\frac{12}{5} + 2\frac{4}{5} =$

_____

5. $1\frac{2}{3} + 1\frac{1}{3} =$

_____

6. $2\frac{1}{4} + 1\frac{3}{4} =$

_____

7. $1\frac{4}{10} + 2\frac{9}{10} =$

_____

8. $1\frac{1}{5} + 1\frac{3}{5} =$

_____

9. $2\frac{1}{6} + 1\frac{4}{6} =$

_____

10. $1\frac{1}{12} + 1\frac{2}{12} =$

_____

11. $3\frac{2}{6} + 1\frac{1}{6} + 1\frac{5}{6} =$

_____

12. $1\frac{1}{2} + 2\frac{1}{2} + 3\frac{1}{2} =$

_____

Solve each problem.

13. After school, Jason has soccer practice for $1\frac{2}{4}$ hours. The drive from soccer practice to home takes $\frac{1}{4}$ hour. Then he spends $1\frac{1}{4}$ hours doing chores before dinner. Draw a model for the problem on another sheet. How much time does Jason spend between school and dinner time?

_____

14. A recipe for brownies calls for $3\frac{2}{3}$ cups of flour and $2\frac{1}{3}$ cups of sugar. How much flour and sugar is needed altogether?

_____

Anna only has a one-third cup measuring cup. How many times must she fill the measuring cup for both the flour and sugar?

_____

CRCT Practice Directions: Choose the best answer for each question.
Circle the letter for the answer you have chosen.

1. Which number sentence belongs with this picture?

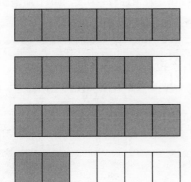

A. $\frac{5}{6} + \frac{2}{6} = \frac{7}{6}$

B. $1\frac{5}{6} + 1\frac{2}{6} = 3\frac{1}{6}$

C. $1\frac{6}{6} + \frac{2}{6} = 2\frac{2}{6}$

D. $2\frac{1}{6} + 1\frac{1}{6} = 3\frac{2}{6}$

2. Which of the following is NOT equivalent to the sum of $1\frac{1}{5} + 1\frac{3}{5}$?

A. $\frac{5}{5}$

B. $\frac{14}{5}$

C. $2\frac{4}{5}$

D. $2\frac{8}{10}$

3. Use the model to find which number goes in the box to make the number sentence true.

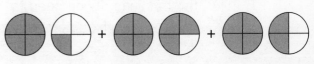

$$1\frac{1}{4} + 1\frac{3}{4} + 1\frac{2}{4} = \boxed{}$$

A. $4\frac{2}{4}$

B. $4\frac{1}{4}$

C. 4

D. $3\frac{3}{4}$

4. Patsy spent $3\frac{5}{6}$ hours reading mystery novels. She also spent $1\frac{3}{6}$ hours reading travel books and $1\frac{1}{6}$ hours reading books about horses. How many hours did Patsy spend reading?

A. five and five-sixths

B. six and one-sixth

C. thirty-nine sixths

D. thirty-six sixths

Lesson 28 Subtract Mixed Numbers

M4N6.b   Add and subtract fractions and mixed numbers with common denominators.

M4N6.c   Convert and use mixed numbers and improper fractions interchangeably.

M4P5   Students will create and use pictures, manipulatives, models, and symbols to organize, record, and communicate mathematical ideas.

You can use models to subtract mixed numbers with common denominators. You can also subtract by subtracting the whole amounts and then subtracting the fractions. If you need to subtract a greater fraction from a lesser fraction, change the mixed numbers to improper fractions and then subtract.

Guided Instruction

Problem

Lisa traveled from New York to Chicago and back. The flight to Chicago took $2\frac{3}{4}$ hours. The flight back to New York took $1\frac{2}{4}$ hours. How much longer was the flight to Chicago?

Step 1   Shade a model to show $2\frac{3}{4}$ hours.

Each whole strip stands for _____ hour.

Each equal part stands for _____ hour.

Step 2   To subtract $1\frac{2}{4}$ hours, cross out one whole strip.
Then cross out two shaded fourths.

Step 3   How many whole strips are left?

$2 - 1 =$ _____

How many shaded fourths are left?

$\frac{3}{4} - \frac{1}{4} =$ _____

Write the parts left as a mixed number. _____

Solution   How much longer was the flight to Chicago? _____ hours

Another Example

Subtract $3\frac{1}{3} - 1\frac{2}{3}$.

Write the mixed numbers as improper fractions.

$3\frac{1}{3} = \frac{10}{3}$ and $1\frac{2}{3} =$ _____

Subtract the improper fractions.

$\frac{10}{3} - \frac{5}{3} = \frac{10 - 5}{3} =$ _____

Write the difference as a mixed number.

$3\frac{1}{3} - 1\frac{2}{3} = \frac{5}{3} =$ _____

      Measuring Up® to the Georgia Performance Standards

Apply the GPS   **Use the models to subtract.**

1.

$1\frac{4}{5} - 1\frac{1}{5} =$ _____

2.

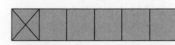
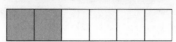

$2\frac{2}{6} - 1\frac{1}{6} =$ _____

3.

$2\frac{1}{3} - 1\frac{2}{3} =$ _____

Subtract. Write each difference as an improper fraction and a mixed number.

4. $7\frac{3}{4} - 5\frac{1}{4} =$

_____

5. $5\frac{5}{12} - 2\frac{1}{12} =$

_____

6. $3\frac{2}{4} - 1\frac{3}{4} =$

_____

7. $6\frac{1}{5} - 1\frac{2}{5} =$

_____

8. $3\frac{1}{8} - 1\frac{3}{8} =$

_____

9. $2\frac{4}{10} - 1\frac{1}{10} =$

_____

10. $3\frac{5}{9} - 1\frac{1}{9} - 1\frac{3}{9} =$

_____

11. $4\frac{3}{4} - 2\frac{1}{4} - 1\frac{1}{4} =$

_____

12. $5\frac{1}{3} - 1\frac{2}{3} - 1\frac{2}{3} =$

_____

Solve each problem.

13. Gary takes the school bus. Linda rides her bike to school. The model shows how long it takes them each to get to school. How much longer does Gary spend traveling than Linda?

_____

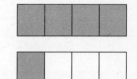

Gary   Linda

14. Douglas has 4 pies to sell. Each pie has 8 slices. He sells 12 slices to his first customer. Then he sells another 10 slices. How much pie is left for him to sell? Write the difference as both an improper fraction and a mixed number.

_____

15. A baseball team played a game that lasted $4\frac{1}{4}$ hours. The next week, the team practiced for $1\frac{1}{4}$ hours and then again for $1\frac{2}{4}$ hours. How much more time did the team spend playing than practicing?

_____

CRCT Practice

Directions: Choose the best answer for each question.
Circle the letter for the answer you have chosen.

1. Which number sentence belongs with this picture?

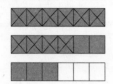

A. $1\frac{3}{6} - \frac{4}{6} = \frac{5}{6}$

B. $2\frac{3}{6} - 1\frac{2}{6} = 1\frac{1}{6}$

C. $2\frac{3}{6} - 1\frac{4}{6} = \frac{5}{6}$

D. $2\frac{4}{6} - 1\frac{3}{6} = 1\frac{1}{6}$

 2. What is three and five-eighths minus one and seven-eighths?

A. twelve-eighths

B. one and four-eighths

C. one and six-eighths

D. two and one-eighths

3. Use the model to find which number makes the number sentence true.

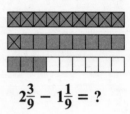

$$2\frac{3}{9} - 1\frac{1}{9} = ?$$

A. $1\frac{2}{9}$

B. $2\frac{1}{9}$

C. $1\frac{4}{9}$

D. $2\frac{4}{9}$

 4. A corn plant grows four and three-fourths feet in a year. A cotton plant grows two and two-fourths feet in a year. How much less does the cotton plant grow than the corn plant?

A. two and three-fourths

B. two and one-fourth

C. one and three-fourths

D. one and one-fourth

Lesson 29 Problem-Solving Strategy: Draw a Picture

M4N6.b   Add and subtract fractions and mixed numbers with common denominators.

M4P1.b   Solve single and multi-step routine word problems related to all appropriate fourth-grade math standards.

M4P5   Students will create and use pictures, manipulatives, models, and symbols to organize, record, and communicate mathematical ideas.

You can draw a picture or a model to help you solve problems.

Guided Instruction

Problem Mindy is making a wood frame for a painting. The painting is $2\frac{3}{4}$ feet wide. Each side of the frame will be $\frac{1}{4}$ foot wide. What will be the total width of the framed painting?

Understand the problem.

What does the problem ask you to find?

_____

_____

Make a plan.

You can draw a picture of the painting and the sides of the frame. Use the picture to find the total width of the framed painting.

Solve the problem.

Draw your picture in the space below. Use the model of one foot divided into 4 equal parts or fourths to help you.

Combine the widths of the painting and the left and right sides of the frame. Count the total number of whole feet and fourths.

What will be the total width of the framed painting? _____

Check your answer.

Did you add $\frac{1}{4}$ for the left side of the frame, $2\frac{3}{4}$ for the painting, and $\frac{1}{4}$ for the right side of the frame? _____

Does your picture show a total width of $3\frac{1}{4}$ feet? _____

Draw a picture or a model to help you solve each problem.

Work Space

1. Olivia swims laps every Saturday. On one Saturday she swam $\frac{4}{10}$ of a mile. The next week she swam $\frac{2}{5}$ of a mile. Did Olivia swim the same distance each week?

   _____

2. Katie pitched $\frac{1}{4}$ of her team's softball game. Melissa pitched $\frac{2}{4}$ of the game. What fraction of the game did Katie and Melissa pitch together?

   _____

3. Jeremy spent $\frac{10}{12}$ of an hour raking leaves. Then he spent $\frac{3}{12}$ of an hour mowing the lawn. How much longer did it take to rake the leaves than to mow the lawn?

   _____

4. Carlos is building a bookshelf with three shelves. The top, middle, and bottom shelves are each $1\frac{1}{2}$ inches thick. Each space between shelves is $8\frac{1}{2}$ inches high. How tall is the bookshelf?

   _____

5. Kim bought 3 cakes for a party. The guests ate $1\frac{5}{8}$ cakes. One guest took $\frac{4}{8}$ of a cake home. How much cake did Kim have left over?

   _____

 Measuring Up® to the Georgia Performance Standards

CRCT Practice   **Directions: Choose the best answer for each question.**
Circle the letter for the answer you have chosen.

1. Which picture shows the sum of the fractions $\frac{2}{6} + \frac{2}{6}$?

    A.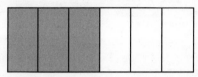

    B.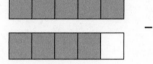

    C.

    D. △ △ △ △

2. Which is the difference of

    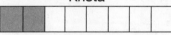 – 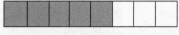 ?

    A. $1\frac{1}{5}$

    B. $1\frac{2}{5}$

    C. $\frac{10}{5}$

    D. $\frac{8}{5}$

3.   To add $1\frac{3}{12}$ and $1\frac{8}{12}$ using a picture, how many shapes must you draw and divide into twelfths?

    A. one

    B. four

    C. eight

    D. twelve

4.   The model shows how many eighths of a mile Alison and Krista live from the beach. How much farther away does Alison live?

    Alison

    Krista

    A. three-eighths

    B. four-eighths

    C. five-eighths

    D. six-eighths

Applying Concepts

Directions: Choose the best answer for each question.

Circle the letter for the answer you have chosen.

 1. Which fraction represents the area that is NOT shaded?

A. $\frac{3}{10}$

B. $\frac{4}{7}$

C. $\frac{7}{10}$

D. $\frac{3}{7}$

2. One of the rides at an amusement park is a roller coaster. A roller coaster car can hold 10 people. The first 6 people in line get into the first car. What fraction of the car is filled?

A. $\frac{4}{10}$

B. $\frac{6}{10}$

C. $\frac{10}{6}$

D. $\frac{10}{4}$

3. Which mixed number is correct?

$$1\frac{1}{4} + \frac{3}{4} + 2\frac{2}{4} =$$

A. $3\frac{2}{4}$

B. $3\frac{3}{4}$

C. $4\frac{2}{4}$

D. $4\frac{3}{4}$

4. Which mixed number is equivalent to the fraction $\frac{10}{3}$?

A. 3

B. $3\frac{1}{3}$

C. $3\frac{2}{3}$

D. $3\frac{3}{3}$

5. Which fraction is NOT equivalent to the fraction shown in the model?

A. $\frac{2}{5}$

B. $\frac{2}{4}$

C. $\frac{3}{6}$

D. $\frac{4}{8}$

6. Brian and Brenda are both serving slices of pie at a bake sale. Brian cuts his pie into four pieces. Brenda cuts hers into eight pieces. Brian sells half of his slices of pie. How many slices must Brenda sell to have half of her pie left?

A. 5 pieces

B. 4 pieces

C. 3 pieces

D. 2 pieces

Copying is illegal.   Measuring Up® to the Georgia Performance Standards

7. Two teams are playing kickball at recess. There are eight students on each team. Half of the students on one team are wearing white sneakers. What fraction of the two teams is NOT wearing white sneakers?

A. $\frac{16}{8}$

B. $\frac{12}{8}$

C. $\frac{12}{16}$

D. $\frac{4}{16}$

8. What fraction names the shaded part?

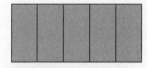

A. $\frac{3}{5}$

B. $\frac{7}{5}$

C. $1\frac{1}{5}$

D. $1\frac{4}{5}$

9. What is the sum of three-sixths and two-sixths?

A. $\frac{5}{6}$

B. $\frac{5}{12}$

C. $\frac{1}{6}$

D. $\frac{1}{12}$

10. What is $\frac{2}{3} + \frac{2}{3} + \frac{1}{3}$?

A. $\frac{5}{9}$

B. $\frac{4}{3}$

C. $1\frac{2}{3}$

D. $2\frac{1}{3}$

11. What is the sum of the fractions?

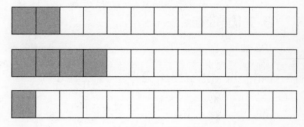

A. $\frac{7}{12}$

B. $\frac{1}{2}$

C. $\frac{6}{24}$

D. $\frac{6}{36}$

12. Linda has $3\frac{1}{4}$ yards of ribbon. She wants to use the ribbon to wrap some presents. She needs $\frac{1}{4}$ yard of ribbon for each present. How many presents can she wrap with the $3\frac{1}{4}$ yards of ribbon?

A. 13

B. 12

C. 8

D. $6\frac{1}{4}$

 13. Six students are working on a puzzle that has a total of 12 pieces. Each student takes $\frac{1}{6}$ of the pieces. Two students place all of their pieces on the puzzle board. How many pieces of the puzzle still need to be added to the puzzle board?

A. 4 pieces

B. 6 pieces

C. 8 pieces

D. 10 pieces

14. Find the difference. $2\frac{7}{10} - 1\frac{4}{10} = ?$

A. $\frac{3}{10}$

B. $1\frac{3}{10}$

C. $1\frac{4}{10}$

D. $1\frac{3}{0}$

15. Three different pizzas are cut into eight slices each. Thomas takes one slice of pepperoni pizza, two slices of mushroom pizza, and one slice of cheese pizza. What fraction of a whole pizza has he taken?

A. $\frac{6}{8}$

B. $\frac{4}{8}$

C. $\frac{3}{8}$

D. $\frac{2}{8}$

16. Rana painted her bedroom blue and purple. The shaded parts in the model show the amounts of paint left. How many more cans of blue paint did she use than cans of purple paint?

 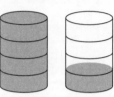

Blue Paint   Purple Paint

A. $\frac{1}{4}$ can

B. $\frac{2}{4}$ can

C. 1 can

D. $1\frac{1}{4}$ cans

17. Which number goes in the box to make the number sentence true: $2\frac{3}{8} + 1\frac{5}{8} = \boxed{} + 2\frac{1}{8}$?

A. $2\frac{1}{8}$

B. 2

C. $1\frac{9}{8}$

D. $1\frac{7}{8}$

18. Which fraction is correct?

$$1 - \frac{1}{7} - \frac{1}{7} - \frac{2}{7} =$$

A. $\frac{3}{7}$

B. $\frac{4}{7}$

C. $\frac{5}{7}$

D. $\frac{6}{7}$

19. Jeremy needs $2\frac{1}{2}$ cups of milk to make pudding. He only has a $\frac{1}{4}$ cup measuring cup. How many times must he fill the measuring cup with milk for the recipe?

    A. 6 times

    B. 8 times

    C. 10 times

    D. 12 times

20. Find the sum.

$$1\frac{1}{10} + \frac{3}{10} + 1\frac{4}{10} =$$

    A. $2\frac{7}{10}$

    B. $2\frac{8}{10}$

    C. $3\frac{1}{30}$

    D. $3\frac{1}{10}$

21. The shaded part of the model shows how much homework Leo finished. Maria finished the same fraction of her homework. She had twice as many problems as Leo. Which fraction shows how much of her homework Maria finished?

    A. $\frac{4}{12}$

    B. $\frac{3}{6}$

    C. $\frac{8}{12}$

    D. $\frac{8}{6}$

22. Which number sentence matches the fraction strips shown below?

    A. $1\frac{3}{9} - 2\frac{1}{9} = 1\frac{1}{9}$

    B. $2\frac{1}{9} - 1\frac{3}{9} = 1\frac{2}{9}$

    C. $2\frac{3}{9} - 1\frac{1}{9} = 1\frac{1}{9}$

    D. $2\frac{3}{9} - 1\frac{1}{9} = 1\frac{2}{9}$

23. What is $6 - 1\frac{2}{4} - 1\frac{1}{4}$?

    A. 2

    B. $2\frac{3}{4}$

    C. 3

    D. $3\frac{1}{4}$

24. Jamal has seven of the twelve cards he needs to win a board game. He picks up one card and wins one card from the person next to him. On the next turn, the player takes away three of Jamal's cards. What fraction of the cards Jamal needs are left in his hand?

    A. $\frac{3}{12}$

    B. $\frac{4}{12}$

    C. $\frac{6}{12}$

    D. $\frac{7}{12}$

Focus on GPS

M4N1.a	Identify place value names and places from hundredths through one million.
M4N5.a	Understand decimal fractions are a part of the base-ten system.
M4P4	Students will understand how mathematical ideas interconnect and build on one another and apply mathematics in other content areas.
M4P5	Students will create and use pictures, manipulatives, models, and symbols to organize, record, and communicate mathematical ideas.

You will learn how a **decimal** uses place value to name a part of a whole. A decimal or decimal fraction is a number that has one or more digits to the right of a decimal point, such as 1.75 or 0.8. Each digit to the right of the decimal point has a different place and value less than one.

Guided Instruction

Problem	Angela bought a box of 100 pens. She used 32 of the pens in the box. What decimal names the part of the box that she used?

Step 1 Look at the model to find the decimal fraction.

How many parts is the square divided into? _____

How many parts are shaded? _____

Write the word form of the decimal.

thirty-two _____

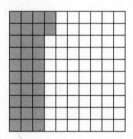

Step 2 Write the number of shaded parts in the place-value chart.

ones	tenths	hundredths
0 .	3	2

What is the place of the digit 3? What is its value? _____

What is the place of the 2? What is its value? _____

Solution	What decimal names the part that Angela used? _____ _____

Another Example

Decimals are also used to show amounts of money. One cent equals one hundredth of a dollar, or $0.01. One whole dollar is written as $1.00.

 $_____

Apply the GPS

Write a decimal for the part that is shaded.

1.

_____

2.

_____

3.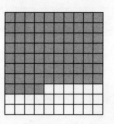

_____

4.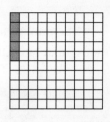

_____

Shade the models to show each decimal. Write the number of parts that you shaded.

5. 0.5

_____

6. 0.48

_____

7. 1.01

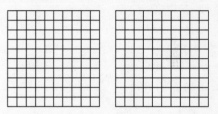

_____

Answer each question.

8. What decimal names the shaded part in this model? What is the place of each digit in the decimal?

_____

_____

9. What is the word name of the decimal 0.64? _____

Complete the chart. Write a decimal for each money amount.

	ones	.	tenths	hundredths
10.				
11.				

Directions: Choose the best answer for each question. Circle the letter for the answer you have chosen.

 1. Which decimal number shows the part of the model that is NOT shaded?

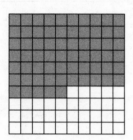

A. 35

B. 65

C. 0.35

D. 0.65

 2. Charlotte has one dollar to spend. She buys a pack of gum for 89 cents. Which decimal shows how much change she should receive?

A. $0.10

B. $0.11

C. $1.00

D. $1.10

3. In the number 2.47, which digit is in the hundredths place?

A. 47

B. 2

C. 4

D. 7

4. Which model shows 0.71?

A.

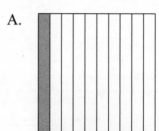

B.

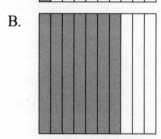

C.

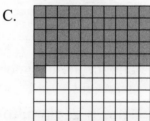

D.

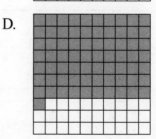

Measuring Up® to the Georgia Performance Standards

Lesson 31 Compare and Order Decimals

M4N5.b Understand the relative size of numbers and order two digit decimal fractions.
M4P3   Students will use the language of mathematics to express ideas precisely.
M4P5   Students will create and use pictures, manipulatives, models, and symbols to organize, record, and communicate mathematical ideas.

You can use models to compare and order decimals. A decimal is greater than another decimal if its model has more parts shaded. Use the symbols > (greater than), < (less than), or = (equal to).

Guided Instruction

| Problem 1 | Box A weighs 0.08 pound. Box B weighs 0.45 pound. Which box weighs more? |

Compare the number of shaded parts in each model.

Write in the correct symbol to show which box has a greater weight.

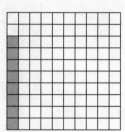   Box A   Box B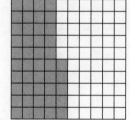

0.08   0.45

| Solution | Which box weighs more? _____ |

| Problem 2 | Which amount of money is greater, $2.50 or $1.75? |

Compare the money amounts and write in the correct symbol.

| Solution | Which amount is greater? _____ |

Another Example

On a number line, the value of decimals increases from left to right.

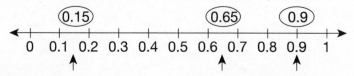

Apply the GPS Use the models to compare. Write >, <, or = for each.

1.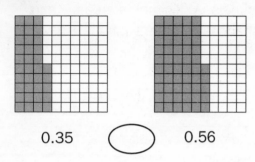

0.35 ◯ 0.56

2.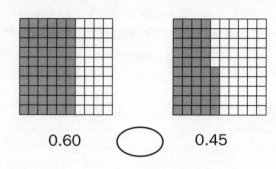

0.60 ◯ 0.45

Use the models to answer questions 3–5. Write the letter of the correct model.

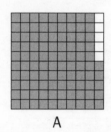 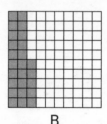 

A   B   C

3. Which model shows a decimal greater than 0.85? _____

4. Which model shows a decimal less than 0.27? _____

5. Which model shows a decimal equal to 0.42? _____

Use the number line to write the decimals in order from least to greatest.

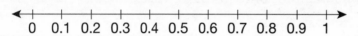

0   0.1   0.2   0.3   0.4   0.5   0.6   0.7   0.8   0.9   1

6. 0.45, 0.25, 0.9 _____

7. 0.40, 0.36, 0.09 _____

Answer each question.

8. Which is greater, 0.72 or 0.27? Shade the models to show each decimal and write the correct symbol.

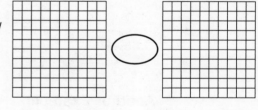

9. Samantha gets two quarters and a dime for allowance. Her brother gets four dimes and two nickels. Who has a greater allowance? Explain.

_____

_____

CRCT Practice Directions: **Choose the best answer for each question. Circle the letter for the answer you have chosen.**

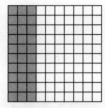 1. Which model shows a decimal that is NOT equal to or greater than 0.30?

A.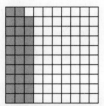

B.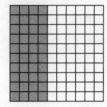

C.

D.

2. Which symbol correctly compares the shaded parts in these models?

 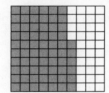

A. >

B. =

C. <

D. +

 3. Which statement is NOT true?

A. 0.29 is greater than 0.19

B. 0.19 is not equal to 0.29

C. 0.19 is greater than 0.29

D. 0.19 is less than 0.29

4. Timothy is choosing a box of chocolates. One box has 0.41 pound of chocolate. The second box has 0.08 pound of chocolate. The third box has 0.50 pound of chocolate. Which box has the GREATEST amount of chocolate?

A. All boxes have the same amount.

B. the box with 0.50 pound

C. the box with 0.08 pound

D. the box with 0.41 pound

Lesson 32 Round Decimals

M4N2.c Understand the meaning of rounding a decimal fraction to the nearest whole number.

M4P1.b Solve single and multi-step routine word problems related to all appropriate fourth-grade math standards.

M4P1.d Determine the most efficient way to solve a problem (mentally, paper/pencil, or calculator).

You can use place value to round decimals to the nearest whole number or any decimal place. Just as when rounding whole numbers, compare the digit to the right of the place you are rounding to to the number 5.

Guided Instruction

Problem

On Monday there was 0.62 inch of rain. What is 0.62 rounded to the nearest whole number? What is 0.62 rounded to the tenths place, or the nearest tenth?

Use place value to round to the ones place and to the tenths place.

Step 1 Write the decimal and underline the digit in the place you are rounding to. To round to the nearest **whole number**, underline the digit in the ones place.

0.62

Step 2 Circle the digit to the right of the underlined place. If the circled digit is 5 or greater, round up. If it is less than 5, round down. When you round down, the digit in the place you are rounding to stays the same.

0.⑥2

Since 6 > 5, round up to the greater whole number. What is the next whole number greater than 0? _____

Now repeat Steps 1 and 2 to round 0.62 to the nearest tenth.

What digit should you circle to round to the tenths place? _____

Should you round up or down? _____

Solution

What is 0.62 rounded to the nearest whole number?

_____ What is 0.62 rounded to the tenths place? _____

Another Example

Elise wants to buy a pen that costs $1.75. She has dollar bills but no change. To bring enough money to the store, what should she round $1.75 to?

Since Elise only has whole dollars, you must round to a whole number amount. Round in your head.

Will $1.00 be enough money to buy the pen? _____

Will $2.00 be enough money to buy the pen? _____

Elise should round $1.75 to the greater whole dollar amount, or _____

Apply the GPS

Round each decimal to the nearest whole number.

1. 0.9 _____

2. 0.4 _____

3. 1.55 _____

4. 0.34 _____

Round each decimal to the nearest tenth.

5. 0.52 _____

6. 0.26 _____

7. 0.47 _____

Round each decimal to the nearest hundredth. Use the place value chart to help you.

ones	tenths	hundredths	thousandths

8. 0.829 _____

9. 0.211 _____

10. 0.594 _____

Round each amount of money to the nearest tenth and nearest whole dollar.

11.  _____

12.  _____

Solve each problem. Use pencil and paper or round in your head.

13. Martha rounded 0.191 to 0.2. Did she round up or down? What place did she round to? _____

14. Victor wants to buy a new pack of baseball cards. The pack of cards cost $2.65. How many dollars must he bring to the store to buy the pack of cards? Explain which method you used and why. _____

_____

_____

CRCT Practice

Directions: Choose the best answer for each question. Circle the letter for the answer you have chosen.

1. Brett measures 4.45 inches of snow outside on his windowsill. What whole number should he use to mark the snowfall amount on his chart?

   A. 4.0

   B. 4.40

   C. 4.50

   D. 5.0

 2. What is the missing digit in the number if the number rounds up to 6.0?

ones	tenths	hundredths
5	—	8

   A. 5

   B. 3

   C. 4

   D. 1

3. Julia goes to the store to buy a new notebook. The notebook costs $1.87. She pays by rounding to the nearest tenth. How much money does she give to the cashier?

   A. $1.00

   B. $1.80

   C. $1.90

   D. $2.00

4. What is the best method for rounding the amount of money shown to the nearest whole dollar?

   A. Write $1.27 on paper. Underline the 2 and compare the 7 to 5.

   B. Write $1.27 on paper. Underline the 1 and compare the 7 to 5.

   C. Think. Compare the amount of money shown to $5.00.

   D. Think. Compare $1.27 to $1.00 and $2.00.

Lesson 33 Add Decimals

M4N5.c	Add and subtract both one and two digit decimal fractions.
M4P1.b	Solve single and multi-step routine word problems related to all appropriate fourth-grade math standards.
M4P3	Students will use the language of mathematics to express ideas precisely.

You can add decimals by combining the shaded parts in decimal models. You can also line up the decimal points and add the same way you add whole numbers.

Guided Instruction

Problem 1

David is going to ride his bike 0.6 mile to school. He will ride 1.5 miles to the baseball field after school. How many miles will he ride his bike today?

Use a model to add the decimals and find the total distance.

Step 1 Shade the model to show each decimal number you are adding.

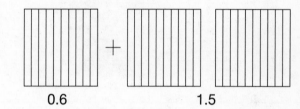

Step 2 Combine the models. What is the total number of shaded parts?

_____

Write the decimal that stands for the combined amount. _____

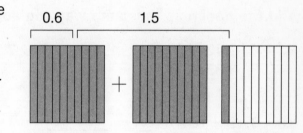

Solution How many miles will David ride his bike today _____ miles

Problem 2 What is the sum of $0.67 + $0.13?

Add the decimals the same way you add whole numbers.

Step 1 Write the decimals in columns. Line up the decimal points as shown.

$$\begin{array}{r} 0.67 \\ + 0.13 \\ \hline \end{array}$$

Step 2 Add the digits in each place. Regroup when needed.

$$\begin{array}{r} {}^{1} \\ 0.67 \\ + 0.13 \\ \hline \end{array}$$

Solution What is the sum of $0.67 and $0.13? _____

Apply the GPS

Use the models to add. Write the sum.

1.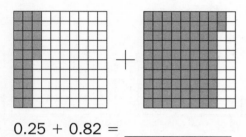

0.3 + 0.5 = _____

2.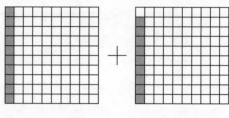

0.1 + 0.09 = _____

3.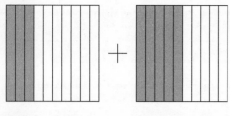

0.25 + 0.82 = _____

4.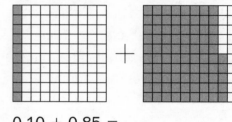

0.10 + 0.85 = _____

Add the decimals the same way you add whole numbers.

5.   0.42
       + 0.35

6.   2.5
       + 0.8

7.   1.9
       + 0.12

8.   0.25
       + 1.30

9.   0.50
       + 0.64

10. 0.12 + 0.47 = _____   **11.** 0.7 + 0.31 = _____

Use the chart to answer questions 12–13.

12. How much will it cost to buy a bottle of juice and a comic book?_____

13. Jamie wants to buy one mint and one chocolate bar. What digit will be in the tenths place in the total price? Explain.

_____

_____

_____

_____

Corner Store Prices

mint	$0.05
chocolate bar	$0.65
juice	$1.39
comic book	$2.75

CRCT
Practice

Directions: Choose the best answer for each question.
Circle the letter for the answer you have chosen.

1. Max runs 1.6 miles around the track at his school. His brother Nate runs 0.82 mile. What is the total distance run by the boys?

   A. 2.42 miles

   B. 2.02 miles

   C. 1.82 miles

   D. 1.42 miles

 2. What sum is shown by the models?

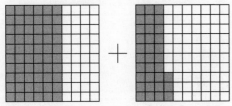

   A. 0.90

   B. 0.93

   C. 1.03

   D. 1.07

3. What is the estimated sum:

   $1.16 + $2.71 = ?

   A. $3.00

   B. $3.50

   C. $4.00

   D. $5.00

 4. Emily is going to the movies. She spends $1.50 for a lemonade and $0.65 for a candy bar. After the movie, she buys a gumball for $0.25. Which of the following is NOT true?

   A. Emily spent a total of $2.40.

   B. Emily spent $2.40 before the movie.

   C. Emily spent $2.15 before the movie.

   D. Emily spent $1.75 on lemonade and a gumball.

M4N5.c	Add and subtract both one and two-digit decimal fractions.
M4P1.b	Solve single and multi-step routine word problems related to all appropriate fourth-grade math standards.
M4P3	Students will use the language of mathematics to express ideas precisely.

You can subtract decimals by crossing out shaded parts in decimal models. You can also line up the decimal points and subtract the same way you subtract whole numbers.

Guided Instruction

Problem   Abigail walks 0.37 of a mile to school and Margaret walks 0.82 of a mile. How much farther does Margaret walk than Abigail?

Use the models to subtract and find the difference in distance.

Step 1   Shade the models to show each decimal number.

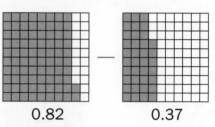

0.82   0.37

Step 2   Cross out to subtract 37 hundredths from 82 hundredths.
How many hundredths are left? _____

Step 3   Write the remaining shaded parts as a decimal.

_____

Solution   How much farther does Margaret walk than Abigail?
_____ of a mile

Another Example

You can also subtract decimals the same way you subtract whole numbers.

Write the decimals in columns. Make sure to line up the decimal points. Then subtract in each place. Regroup when needed.

$$
\begin{array}{r}
{\scriptstyle 7\ 12}\\
0.8\,\cancel{2}\\
+\ 0.3\ 7\\
\hline
0.4\ 5
\end{array}
$$

0.82 − 0.47 = _____

Apply the GPS

Use the models to subtract. Write the difference.

1.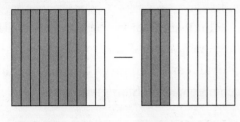

_____

2.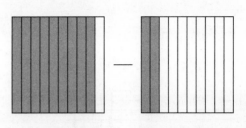

_____

3.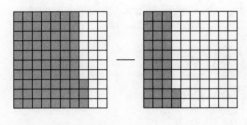

_____

4.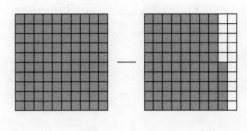

_____

Subtract the same way you subtract whole numbers.

5.   0.4
      − 0.2

6.   0.07
      − 0.03

7.   0.67
      − 0.31

8.   0.9
      − 0.08

9. $0.70
      − $0.24

10. $1.55
       − $0.65

Answer each question.

11. Marla goes into the post office. She buys a book of stamps for $3.45 and an envelope that costs $0.30. She gives the clerk $5.00. How much change will she get back? _____

12. Chris is comparing the amount of snowfall for last year and this year. Last year there was 12.83 inches of snowfall. How much did it snow this year if the total snowfall was 0.60 inch less than last year? _____
What if the snowfall was 0.06 inch less than last year? _____
Explain why it is important to line up the decimals before subtracting.

_____

_____

CRCT
Practice

Directions: Choose the best answer for each question.
Circle the letter for the answer you have chosen.

1. Use the models to subtract:

$$0.5 - 0.19 = ?$$

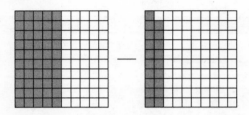

   A. 0.14

   B. 0.24

   C. 0.31

   D. 0.41

2. Beth is planning to walk to the shopping mall. The mall is 2.14 miles from her house. She walks 1.27 miles and stops for a rest. How much farther does she have to walk to reach the mall?

   A. 0.13 mile

   B. 0.31 mile

   C. 0.41 mile

   D. 0.87 mile

3. Sam is selling some of his baseball cards. He is selling them at $0.85 a card. Lucas buys two baseball cards and gives Sam $2.00. How much change should Sam give Lucas?

   A.

   B.

   C.

   D.

4. Find the difference:

$$0.61 - 0.25 = ?$$

   A. 0.46

   B. 0.36

   C   0.35

   D. 0.25

Lesson 35 Multiply a Decimal by a Whole Number

M4N5.d Model multiplication and division of decimal fractions by whole numbers.

M4N5.e Multiply and divide both one and two-digit decimal fractions by whole numbers.

M4P5 Students will create and use pictures, manipulatives, models, and symbols to organize, record, and communicate mathematical ideas.

You can use models to help you multiply decimals by whole numbers. You can also multiply the same way you multiply whole numbers. The product should have the same number of decimal places as the decimal factor.

Guided Instruction

Problem A cookie recipe calls for 0.75 cup of sugar for one batch of cookies. How much sugar does Andrew need to make three batches of cookies?

Use models to multiply or combine equal decimal amounts.

Step 1 Write the multiplication problem. How many batches of cookies does Andrew want to make? 0.75 × _____

sugar for 1 batch

Step 2 Use models to show the multiplication as repeated addition.

1st batch + 2nd batch + 3rd batch

Step 3 Combine the models to find the product or total amount.

0.75 × 3 = _____

Solution How much sugar does Andrew need for three batches of cookies? _____ cups

Another Example

Anita has three nickels. How much money does she have?

Multiply the same way you multiply whole numbers.

$$\begin{array}{r} \overset{1}{\$0.0\underline{5}} \\ \times 3 \\ \hline \$0.1\underline{5} \end{array}$$

Count the number of decimal places in 0.05, the decimal factor. Put the same number of decimal places in the product.

Apply the GPS

Use models to multiply. Write each product.

1.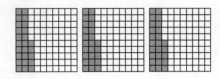

0.25 × 3 = _____

2.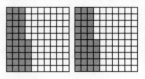

0.35 × 2 = _____

3.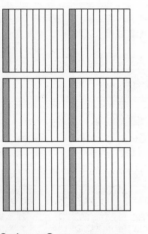

0.1 × 6 = _____

4.

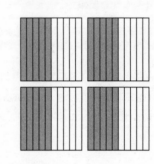

0.5 × 4 = _____

Multiply. Use models or multiply the same way you multiply whole numbers.

5. 0.15 × 4 = _____

6. 0.08 × 11 = _____

7. 0.5 × 12 = _____

8. $0.20 × 7 = _____

9. $0.45 × 3 = _____

10. $0.50 × 9 = _____

Draw a model and multiply.

11. Maria eats a granola bar every day after school. One granola bar costs $0.35. She buys 5 bars for the week. Write the multiplication sentence for the problem and solve. How much money does she spend?

CRCT Practice

Directions: Choose the best answer for each question.

Circle the letter for the answer you have chosen.

1. Which model shows the product of 0.41×3?

   A.

   B.

   C.

   D.

2. A box of twelve cupcakes costs $1.20 at the store. Andrea wants to buy two boxes for her craft club. How much money will two boxes cost?

   A. $2.40

   B. $2.20

   C. $1.20

   D. $0.60

3. Gregory goes to the post office to mail 4 letters. Each letter will cost $0.42 to mail. How much money does Gregory need to mail all 4 letters?

   A. $16.80

   B. $1.68

   C. $1.42

   D. $1.16

4. What problem is modeled below?

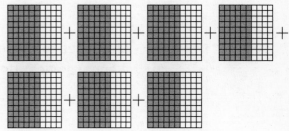

   A. 0.6×7

   B. $0.6 + 7$

   C. $0.6 + 0.6 + 0.6 + 0.6 + 0.6 + 0.6$

   D. $0.6 \div 7$

Lesson 36 Divide a Decimal by a Whole Number

M4N5.d Model multiplication and division of decimal fractions by whole numbers.
M4N5.e Multiply and divide both one and two-digit decimal fractions by whole numbers.
M4P5 Students will create and use pictures, manipulatives, models, and symbols to organize, record, and communicate mathematical ideas.

You can use models to help you divide some decimals by whole numbers. You can also divide the same way you divide whole numbers. The quotient should have the same number of decimal places as the dividend.

Guided Instruction

Problem

A team of 4 students is running a relay race at school. The total distance for the race is 0.8 mile. If each student on the team runs an equal part of the race, how far will each student run?

Step 1 Write the division problem.
How many equal parts do you need to divide 0.8 into?

0.8 ÷ _____

Step 2 Shade a model to show the decimal you are dividing.

Step 3 Draw lines to divide or separate the 8 tenths into 4 equal groups. How many tenths are in each equal group?

0.8 ÷ 4 = _____

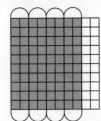

Solution How far will each student on the team run? _____

Another Example

Santo has $1.20. He can buy four pencils with this money.
How much does each pencil cost?

You can divide as you would with whole numbers.
Place the decimal point in the quotient directly above the
decimal point in the dividend. Then divide.

$$\begin{array}{r} 0.30 \\ 4\overline{)1.20} \\ -1.2 \\ \hline 0 \end{array}$$

How much does each pencil cost? _____

Apply the GPS

Use the models to divide. Write each quotient.

1.

0.9 ÷ 3 = _____

2.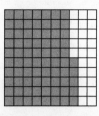

0.75 ÷ 3 = _____

3.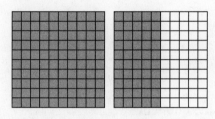

1.50 ÷ 6 = _____

4.

0.25 ÷ 5 = _____

Divide. Use models or divide the same way you divide whole numbers.

5. 0.90 ÷ 3 = _____

6. 0.08 ÷ 4 = _____

7. 1.05 ÷ 5 = _____

8. 0.44 ÷ 11 = _____

9. $2.25 ÷ 9 = _____

10. $0.45 ÷ 9 = _____

Draw a model to solve each problem. Write a division sentence for each.

11. Alex has $0.63 in his coin bank. He wants to buy 9 mints to share with his friends after school. If he uses all of the money to buy the 9 mints, how much does each mint cost?

12. Dennis takes 5 identical packages to the post office. Together the packages weigh 0.95 pound. How much does each package weigh?

_____

_____

CRCT Practice

Directions: Choose the best answer for each question.

Circle the letter for the answer you have chosen.

1. Which of the following shows the solution to the problem:

$$0.75 \div 3 = ?$$

A.

B.

C.

D.

2. Solve:

$$0.6 \div 6 = ?$$

A. one and one tenth

B. one

C. one tenth

D. one hundredth

 3. Melissa has $1.60 in change. She wants to divide the change into piles of equal amounts. Which of the following could NOT be the amount of money in one pile?

A. $0.20

B. $0.40

C. $0.60

D. $0.80

4. Which is the quotient

$$2\overline{)3.66}$$

A. 1.83

B. 0.83

C. 0.183

D. 0.08

Lesson 37 Problem-Solving Strategy: Use a Model

M4N5.a	Understand decimal fractions are a part of the base-ten system.
M4P1.b	Solve single and multi-step routine word problems related to all appropriate fourth-grade math standards.
M4P5	Students will create and use pictures, manipulatives, models, and symbols to organize, record, and communicate mathematical ideas.

Drawing a model of a problem can help you to find the answer.

Guided Instruction

Problem

Alice is putting pictures from her vacation into a large photo album. Each page of the album holds 10 photos. Alice has put the first 4 photos on the first page. What decimal names the part of the page she has filled with photos?

Understand the problem.

Each page holds _____ photos.

Each photo represents 1 _____ of the whole page.

Make a plan.

You can draw a model to show the page in the photo album. Use the model to figure out how many tenths of the page are filled with photos.

Solve the problem.

Draw a tenths model. Shade 4 columns for the 4 photos that Alice has added to the page.

What does each column hold? _____

How many columns are shaded? _____

What decimal names the shaded part in the model? _____

What decimal names the part of the page she has filled with photos? _____

Check your answer.

Does the model you drew show the value of the decimal 0.4? _____

Apply the GPS

Draw a model to help you solve each problem.

Work Space

1. Leo is running a 10-km race in the park. He runs for about an hour. At the end of the hour he has run 4 km. What decimal stands for the part of the race Leo has left to run?

   _____

2. Irene is buying ribbon to decorate a package. The ribbon costs $0.85 for each meter. Irene wants to buy 4 meters of the ribbon. How much will the ribbon cost?

   _____

3. Lisa is building a tree house. She has one wooden board that is 5.20 feet long. She needs to saw the board into 10 smaller pieces that are the same length. How long should each of the 10 pieces be?

   _____

4. Mark keeps a log of the time he spends doing homework each day. On Monday, he studied spelling words for 0.5 hour. Then he spent 1.25 hours doing math problems. How many hours of homework did Mark do on Monday?

   _____

5. Edward is counting up his allowance. He received $1.80 for the week. Then he went to the store and bought a sticker for $0.25. How much money does Edward have left?

   _____

CRCT Practice   **Directions: Choose the best answer for each question.**
Circle the letter for the answer you have chosen.

1. Which model is shaded to show 0.75?

   A.

   B.

   C.

   D.

2. Which decimal shows the difference of the decimals modeled below?

   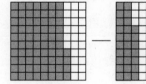

   A. 1.01
   B. 0.74
   C. 0.57
   D. 0.47

3. Which amount of money is shown by the shaded part of the model?

   A. $1.82
   B. $0.87
   C. $0.43
   D. $0.13

4. Daniel walks 0.4 mile to school. Then he walks 0.23 mile to the park before walking 0.1 mile home. How far has he walked?

   A. 0.73 mile
   B. 0.63 mile
   C. 0.5 mile
   D. 43 miles

Directions: Choose the best answer for each question.
Circle the letter for the answer you have chosen.

1. What is the place of the 4 in 1.643?

   A. ones

   B. tenths

   C. hundredths

   D. thousandths

2. What decimal matches the model?

   A. 0.05

   B. 0.5

   C. 5.0

   D. 50.0

3. Four amounts of money are on a counter. The amounts are $2.25, $1.25, $0.89, and $0.65. Which amount has the greatest value in the tenths place?

   A. $0.65

   B. $0.89

   C. $1.25

   D. $2.25

4. Which numbers are in order from least to greatest?

   A. 0.80, 0.65, 0.40, 0.05

   B. 0.25, 0.21, 0.55, 0.07

   C. 0.6, 0.09, 0.45, 0.84

   D. 0.08, 0.60, 0.72, 0.95

5. Donna has ten dimes. Three of the dimes are new coins. Which amount shows the value of the dimes that are new?

   A. $0.30

   B. $0.03

   C. $3.00

   D. $0.70

6. Which symbol belongs in the ☐ to make the number sentence true?

   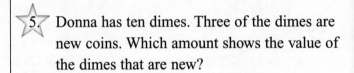

   A. =

   B. −

   C. <

   D. >

7. Which number shows the amount below rounded to the nearest whole dollar?

A. $1.00

B. $1.30

C. $1.40

D. $2.00

8. What is the sum of the expression?

$$0.12 + 0.28 + 0.40 =$$

A. 0.60

B. 0.68

C. 0.70

D. 0.80

9. A thermometer shows the temperature outside is 88.65 degrees. If the temperature falls by 5.5 degrees, what is the new temperature?

A. 83.15 degrees

B. 83.60 degrees

C. 88.15 degrees

D. 88.6 degrees

10. At the movies, Kelly bought some popcorn and a drink. The total cost was $8.38. She paid $9.00 to the cashier. How many pennies should she get back?

A. one

B. two

C. four

D. eight

11. Matt is adding up the rainfall for one week. On four different days, the town received 0.6, 0.25, 0.09, and 1.15 inches of rain. About how many whole inches of rain did the town get?

A. 1.9

B. 2.5

C. 2.0

D. 1.1

12. Anna wrote the decimal 0.47 as 0.74. Which of the following does NOT describe how she changed the value of 0.47?

A. She added 3 tenths.

B. She subtracted 3 tenths.

C. She subtracted 3 hundredths.

D. She wrote a greater amount.

13. Stanley is buying some snacks at the store. He spends $1.45 on licorice and $0.75 on gum. Then he buys 2 bags of jellybeans for $0.35 each. How much money does he spend altogether?

   A. $2.90

   B. $1.95

   C. $1.90

   D. $1.80

14. Andrea takes $5.00 out of her savings bank. She spends $2.25 on a book. Then she spends $1.45 on a pen and $0.80 on a pad of paper. How much money does she have left?

   A. $1.75

   B. $1.50

   C. $0.50

   D. $0.05

15. Subtract 0.34 from 0.8. What digit is now in the hundredths place?

   A. 4

   B. 6

   C. 5

   D. 1

16. Which symbol shows the relationship between the sums?

   $$0.23 + 0.31 \boxed{} 0.33 + 0.28$$

   A. =

   B. (

   C. <

   D. >

17. Find the difference.

   $$0.71 - 0.22 =$$

   A. 0.41

   B. 0.49

   C. 0.59

   D. 0.93

18. Which equation matches the model?

   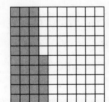 

   A. $0.30 \times 2 = 0.60$

   B. $0.20 \times 35 = 0.70$

   C. $0.35 + 2 = 0.37$

   D. $0.35 \times 2 = 0.70$

19. Tisha takes the city bus from school to the gym where she plays volleyball. She takes the bus 5 times a week. The bus costs $0.85 a ride. Which expression shows how much money she spends each week?

    A. 0.85 + 5

    B. 0.85 + 0.35

    C. 0.85 × 5

    D. 0.85 × 5

20. If you divide the shaded area in the model by ten, what will be the value of the shaded area?

    A. ten hundredths

    B. one hundredth

    C. ten tenths

    D. one

21. Miguel buys his lunch at school. On four days he buys a hamburger for $1.75. On one day he buys a hot dog for $1.10. About how much money does Miguel spend on lunch for the five days?

    A. $7.00

    B. $9.00

    C. $10.00

    D. $11.00

22. What is the solution to the problem shown in the model?

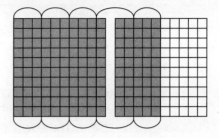

    A. 0.20

    B. 0.25

    C. 0.30

    D. 0.50

23. Which decimal is correct?

    $$1.20 \div 6 =$$

    A. 0.40

    B. 0.30

    C. 0.25

    D. 0.20

24. Lupe is going to ride her bike 9.60 miles on Saturday. She will stop three times during the ride. If she bikes the same distance before each stop, how far will Lupe ride between each stop?

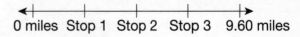

0 miles   Stop 1   Stop 2   Stop 3   9.60 miles

    A. 3.30 miles

    B. 3.20 miles

    C. 2.60 miles

    D. 2.25 miles

Lesson 38 **Create and Extend Patterns**

M4A1.a Understand and apply patterns and rules to describe relationships and solve problems.

M4P1.c Determine the operation(s) needed to solve a problem.

M4P5 Students will create and use pictures, manipulatives, models, and symbols to organize, record, and communicate mathematical ideas.

You can make, extend, and use patterns to solve problems. Patterns can be shown using numbers, figures, or objects.

Guided Instruction

Problem

Miguel puts quarters in his savings bank every week. Using the pattern shown below, how many quarters will he have by the fourth and fifth weeks?

Week 1	Week 2	Week 3	Week 4	Week 5
			?	?

Step 1 What is the difference between the number of quarters for Week 1 and Week 2? _____

What is the difference between the number of quarters for Week 2 and Week 3? _____

Step 2 How many quarters does Miguel add each week? _____

Step 3 Use the pattern to find the number of quarters for Weeks 4 and 5.

Week 4: _____ + 2 = _____

Week 5: _____ + 2 = _____

Solution How many quarters will Miguel have by the fourth and fifth weeks? _____

Other Examples

You can pattern to multiply by 10 or multiples of 10.

1 × 10 = _____   6 × 1 = _____

2 × 10 = _____   6 × 10 = _____

3 × 10 = _____   6 × 100 = _____

Apply the GPS

Use the models to complete each pattern.

1.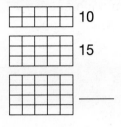

5
10
15
_____

$5 \times 5 =$ _____

2.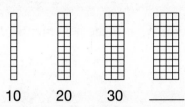

10   20   30   _____

$10 \times 5 =$ _____

$10 \times 6 =$ _____

Use a pattern of zeros to find the products.

3. $2 \times 1 =$ _____

$2 \times 10 =$ _____

$2 \times 100 =$ _____

4. $5 \times 1 =$ _____

$5 \times 10 =$ _____

$5 \times 100 =$ _____

5. $7 \times 1 =$ _____

$7 \times 10 =$ _____

$7 \times 100 =$ _____

Use the rule to write the next two numbers in each pattern.

6. Add 6.

1, 7, 13, 19, _____, _____

7. Multiply by 2, then subtract 4.

6, 8, 12, 20, _____, _____

Write the missing numbers in each pattern.

8. 2, 4, 8, 16, _____, 64, _____

10. 45, 52, 59, 66, _____, _____

9. 74, 64, 54, 44, _____, _____

11. 224, 112, 56, 28, _____, _____

Describe each pattern.

12. 1, 5, 21, 85, 341

_____

13. 100, 85, 70, 55, 40

_____

14. What pattern is shown by the model? Explain.

_____

_____

_____

_____

_____

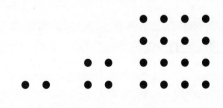

CRCT Practice

Directions: Choose the best answer for each question. Circle the letter for the answer you have chosen.

1. Look at this pattern. What is the next number?

△ △ △ △ △
△ △ △ △ △ △ △ △ △ △
△ △ △ △ △ △ △ △ △ △ △ △ △ △ △
△ △ △ △ △ △ △ △ △ △ △ △ △ △ △
   10   △ △ △ △ △ △ △ △ △ △
        20   △ △ △ △ △
            30

A. 50

B. 40

C. 30

D. 20

2. Look at this pattern. What operation is used to find each number?

1 ☐ 3 = 4
2 ☐ 3 = 5
3 ☐ 3 = 6

A. +

B. −

C. ×

D. ÷

3. Use this rule to find the missing number: divide by 4, then subtract 2.

20 → 3

40 →

A. 30

B. 10

C. 8

D. 6

4. To play a board game, you must roll a dice to move your game piece. The rule is to multiply the number rolled by 2, and then add 1. If Sam rolls a 5, how many places can he move his game piece?

A. 5

B. 10

C. 11

D. 9

Lesson 39 Determine the Rule

M4A1.a   Understand and apply patterns and rules to describe relationships and solve problems.
M4P1.c   Determine the operation(s) needed to solve a problem.

You can find the rule for the numbers in an input/output table by looking for a pattern. The **rule** tells you how the numbers in a pattern change, or how they are related. If the "Out" numbers are greater than the "In" numbers, the rule may use addition or multiplication. If the "Out" numbers are less than the "In" numbers, the rule may use subtraction or division.

Guided Instruction

Problem	Marta wants to know how much water drips from her kitchen faucet. She made a table to show how much water dripped into a bucket in the sink. Based on this pattern, how much water will drip in 6 hours?

Hours	Quarts
1	3
2	6
3	9
4	12

Find and use the rule for the table.

Step 1   Compare the "Out" numbers (quarts) to the "In" numbers (hours).

Are the numbers of quarts greater than or less than the numbers of hours? _____

What operations should you try? _____

Step 2   Try both operations for each pair of numbers.

Add   Multiply

$1 + \underline{\hspace{1cm}} = 3$ $1 \times \underline{\hspace{1cm}} = 3$

$2 + \underline{\hspace{1cm}} = 6$ $2 \times \underline{\hspace{1cm}} = 6$

$3 + \underline{\hspace{1cm}} = 9$ $3 \times \underline{\hspace{1cm}} = 9$

$4 + \underline{\hspace{1cm}} = 12$ $4 \times \underline{\hspace{1cm}} = 12$

What can you do to each "In" number to get the "Out" number?

_____

Step 3   Use the rule to solve the problem.

How many hours will the water drip? _____

Write a number sentence and solve the problem. _____

Solution	How much water will drip in 6 hours? _____

Apply the GPS

Find the rule for the pairs of numbers in each table.

1.

In	Out
3	8
4	9
5	10
6	11

Rule: _____

2.

In	Out
2	8
3	12
4	16
5	20

Rule: _____

Find the rule. Then complete each table.

3. Rule: _____

_____

Cost of Shared Snacks

Total cost	Cost per student
$3	$1
$6	
	$3
$12	
	$5

4. Rule: _____

_____

Group Discounts for Movie Tickets

People in group	Total cost of tickets
4	30
6	46
8	
	78
12	

Use the table to the right to answer questions 5–6.

5. David is making lemonade for his school picnic. What rule should he follow to use the right amounts of sugar and water for the lemonade?

_____

_____

Cups of Sugar	Quarts of Water
1	2
2	4
3	6
4	8

6. David needs to make more than 8 quarts of lemonade. Write the next larger amounts of sugar and water that he can use in the table. Explain how you found each number.

_____

_____

Directions: Choose the best answer for each question. Circle the letter for the answer you have chosen.

 1. Which expression shows the rule for the table below?

64	16
32	8
24	6

A. $n + 4$

B. $n - 4$

C. $n \times 4$

D. $n \div 4$

 2. If each row of toothpicks has 3 fewer toothpicks than the row below it, how many toothpicks would be needed for the fifth row?

A. 9

B. 12

C. 15

D. 18

3. Look at the pairs of numbers in the table below. What rule can you apply to each "In" number to get each "Out" number?

In	Out
1	1
2	3
3	5

A. add 2

B. multiply by 2

C. multiply by 2 and add 1

D. multiply by 2 and subtract 1

4. A camp charges $6 for a campsite on the first night. Each night after that, the site costs $1 more. What will be the total cost of camping out for 4 nights?

A. $48

B. $30

C. $18

D. $12

Lesson 40 Relate Operations

M4A1.a	Understand and apply patterns and rules to describe relationships and solve problems.
M4N7.a	Describe situations in which the four operations may be used and the relationships among them.
M4P1.b	Solve single and multi-step routine word problems related to all appropriate fourth-grade math standards.
M4P1.c	Determine the operation(s) needed to solve a problem.

You can use related operations to help you solve problems. Multiplication and division are opposite operations that give you numbers from the same fact family. Addition and subtraction are also opposite operations. Multiplication and addition are related in a different way. You can use multiplication facts to help you add the same amount many times.

Guided Instruction

Problem 1

Kyle bought hamburger buns for a cookout. Each package has 8 buns. If Kyle bought a total of 40 hamburger buns, how many packages did he buy?

Use multiplication facts to help you divide.

Step 1 Write a division sentence for the problem.

$\underline{\hspace{1cm}} \div 8 = ?$

Step 2 Think of a related multiplication fact to help you divide.

8 times what number equals 40?

$8 \times \underline{\hspace{1cm}} = 40$ so $40 \div 8 = \underline{\hspace{1cm}}$.

Solution

How many packages of buns did Kyle buy? $\underline{\hspace{2cm}}$

Problem 2

Deepa bought 5 packages of juice boxes. Each package has 4 boxes of juice. How many juice boxes did she buy altogether

Use multiplication facts to help you add.

Step 1 Write an addition sentence for the problem.

$\underline{\hspace{1cm}} + \underline{\hspace{1cm}} + \underline{\hspace{1cm}} + \underline{\hspace{1cm}} + \underline{\hspace{1cm}} = ?$

Step 2 Think of a related multiplication fact to help you add.

$4 \times 5 = \underline{\hspace{1cm}}$ so $\underline{\hspace{1cm}} + \underline{\hspace{1cm}} + \underline{\hspace{1cm}} + \underline{\hspace{1cm}} + \underline{\hspace{1cm}} = \underline{\hspace{1cm}}$

Solution

How many juice boxes did Deepa buy? $\underline{\hspace{1cm}}$

Measuring Up® to the Georgia Performance Standards

Apply the GPS

Complete the related number sentences for each problem.

1. 3 + 7 = 10

10 − _____ = 3

2. 4 × 12 = 48

48 ÷ 4 = _____

3. 2 + 2 + 2 + 2 = 8

2 × _____ = 8

4. 6 + 6 + 6 = 18

6 × _____ = 18

5. 15 − 9 = 6

6 + _____ = 15

6. 50 ÷ _____ = 10

5 × _____ = 50

7. 6 × 6 = _____

36 ÷ 6 = _____

8. 35 ÷ 7 = _____

5 × _____ = 35

9. _____ + 25 = 60

60 − 25 = _____

Use a related operation to find the missing numbers.

10. _____ + 17 = 25

11. _____ − 24 = 24

12. 9 × _____ = 27

13. _____ × 9 = 18

14. 64 ÷ _____ = 16

15. _____ ÷ 9 = 6

Solve each problem.

16. Barry buys 1 pack of baseball cards each week. Each pack has 8 cards. How many cards will Barry have after 6 weeks? Write two number sentences to show two ways of finding the solution.

_____

17. Alice is 35 years old. She is also 21 years older than Michael. What operation can you use to find out how old Michael is? _____

What is a related operation that can help you?

_____

Write the number sentence for the problem and solve.

_____

18. Chang bought three boxes of doughnuts for his class party. He bought a total of 36 doughnuts. How many doughnuts were in each box? _____

19. Fred is passing pencils out to the class before a test. He has 48 pencils in a box. Each student gets 2 pencils. If he hands out all of the pencils, how many students are in the class? _____

CRCT Practice   **Directions: Choose the best answer for each question. Circle the letter for the answer you have chosen.**

 1. Which fact can help you find out how many groups of 2 stars can be made from the stars below?

   A. $2 + 10 = 12$

   B. $12 - 10 = 2$

   C. $3 \times 4 = 12$

   D. $2 \times 6 = 12$

2. What is the missing factor?

$$9 \times \boxed{} = 81$$

   A.   72

   B.   9

   C.   10

   D.   90

3. Two operations can be used to combine small amounts into one large amount. Which of these is the opposite of division?

   A.   subtraction

   B.   addition

   C.   multiplication

   D.   comparing

 4. A school bus holds 60 students. There are 2 sections of seats on the bus. Each section has 10 rows of seats. Which number sentence shows the number of students in each section and the number of students on each seat?

   A. $30 \div 10 = 3$

   B. $60 \div 10 = 6$

   C. $20 \times 3 = 60$

   D. $30 + 30 = 60$

M4A1.a   Understand and apply patterns and rules to describe relationships and solve problems.
M4P1.c   Determine the operation(s) needed to solve a problem.

You will learn how to use the order of operations below to solve problems.

Order of Operations

1. Do operations shown in parentheses or ( ).

2. Multiply and divide from left to right in the problem.

3. Add and subtract from left to right in the problem.

Guided Instruction

| Problem |

Alan has 6 boxes of yellow tennis balls. Each box holds 5 balls. He also has one box of 5 orange balls. If Allan gives away 3 balls, hom many balls will be left altogether? To find out, use the order of operations to solve the number sentence:

$$(6 \times 5) + 5 - 3 = ?$$

Step 1   Do the operation in parentheses first.

$(6 \times 5) + 5 - 3 = ? \longrightarrow 6 \times 5 = $ _____

Rewrite the number sentence using the product you found.

_____ $+ 5 - 3 = ?$

Step 2   Multiply and divide from left to right.

Do you need to multiply or divide here? _____

Step 3   Add and subtract from left to right.

$30 + 5 - 3 = ? \longrightarrow 30 + 5 = $ _____

Rewrite the number sentence using the new sum.

_____ $- 3 = ?$

Subtract to finish the problem.

$35 - 3 = $ _____

| Solution | How many balls will be left altogether? _____

Another Example

$5 + \mathbf{7} \times \mathbf{3} \longrightarrow 7 \times 3 = 21$

$5 + \mathbf{21} = 26$

Apply the GPS

Write the first step in solving each problem.

1. $3 \times 6 + 4$

_____

2. $(13 - 5) \times 2$

_____

3. $5 + 7 \times 3$

_____

4. $25 \div 5 - 4$

_____

5. $45 \div (12 - 3) \times 5$

_____

6. $5 + 7 - 2 + 15 - 4$

_____

Use the order of operations to solve.

7. $5 \times 5 - 3 =$ _____

8. $(3 + 8) \times 5 =$ _____

9. $24 \div 2 - 7 =$ _____

10. $2 \times 6 + 2 - 4 =$ _____

11. $(4 - 2) \times (3 + 3) =$ _____

12. $(21 \div 3) \times 4 - 5 =$ _____

Solve each number sentence and compare. Write the correct symbol in the box.

13. $12 \div 4 + 2 \boxed{} 2 + 4 - 1$

14. $10 - 4 \times (5 - 3) \boxed{} 10 \times 2 \div 4$

15. $9 \times 3 + 2 - (7 + 5) \boxed{} 15 + (30 \div 3)$

16. $(17 + 6 - 2) \div 7 \boxed{} 2 + 6 + 14 \div 7$

Solve each problem.

17. Work from left to right to solve the problem. Write each step in the problem in the correct order.

$(6 \times 3 + 8 \div 4) \times (3 + 2) - 1 =$ _____

_____

_____

_____

18. Joshua is playing a game. He collects 5 cards that are worth 8 points each. Then he loses 2 cards that are worth 3 points each, and gets 1 card that is worth 9 points. How many points does he have?

$5 \times 8 - 2 \times 3 + 9 =$ _____ points

CRCT Practice   **Directions: Choose the best answer for each question.**
Circle the letter for the answer you have chosen.

 1. Which expression shows the BEST method for solving the following word problem?

> Alice scored 80 points on Test 1, 91 points on Test 2, and 96 points on Test 3. Cathy scored the same number of points as Alice on Test 1. She scored 5 points less than Alice on Test 2, and half as many points as Alice on Test 3. How many points did Cathy score on all three tests combined?

A. $80 + 91 + 96 \div 2 - 5$

B. $80 + (91 - 5) + (96 \div 2)$

C. $(80 \times 2) + 91 + (96 \div 2)$

D. $80 - 5 + (91 + 96) \div 2$

2. What is the first step in solving this problem?

$$36 \div 3 - 4 + (8 \div 8) \times 6$$

A. 1×6

B. 8×6

C. $36 \div 3$

D. $8 \div 8$

 3. Which symbol belongs in the ☐ to make a true number sentence?

$$15 \times 2 - 8 \ \boxed{} \ 2 \times (41 - 30)$$

A. $=$

B. $\neq$

C. $<$

D. $>$

4. Nathan is collecting cans for his school's recycling drive. He picks up 4 cases of cans. Each case has 12 cans. Then he finds 8 more cans and gives 9 cans to his little brother to recycle. How many cans does Nathan have?

A. 51

B. 17

C. 47

D. 71

Lesson 42 Write and Evaluate Mathematical Expressions

M4A1.b	Represent unknowns using symbols, such as △ and ☐.
M4A1.c	Write and evaluate mathematical expressions using symbols and different values.
M4P1.b	Solve single and multi-step routine word problems related to all appropriate fourth-grade math standards.

You can write an expression to describe an amount. An **expression** uses numbers, operations, and symbols or letters called **variables**. A variable is any symbol or letter that stands for an unknown amount. When you replace the variables in an expression with numbers, you can evaluate or solve the expression.

Guided Instruction

Problem 1   Alan bought 4 new shirts for school. The next day, he bought a few more. How many shirts did Alan buy in all?

Use the variable △ to write an expression for the problem.

Step 1   Identify what you do and do not know.

How many shirts did Alan buy? _____

What is the unknown amount in the problem?

_____

Step 2   Let △ stand for the unknown number of extra shirts.

Write an expression to describe the total number of shirts Alan bought. 4 + _____

Solution   How many shirts did Alan buy? _____

Problem 2   Leo lost *x* out of 100 marbles. How many marbles are left if *x* =

Write an expression and use the different values for *x* to solve.

Step 1   How many marbles does Leo start with? _____

What does the variable *x* stand for?

_____

Step 2   Use *x* to write an expression for the number of marbles left. 100 − _____

Step 3   Replace *x* with the given value and solve.

$x = 10 \longrightarrow 100 - x = 100 - 10 = 90$

Solution   How many marbles are left if x = 10? _____

       Measuring Up® to the Georgia Performance Standards

Apply the GPS

Use the variable △ to write an expression for each problem.

1. Lillian runs several miles at the track after school. Amanda runs 2 miles more than Lillian. How far does Amanda run?

_____

2. Jonathan picks 20 apples from an apple tree in his backyard. How many apples are left on the tree?

_____

3. Anna and Maki are fishing. Maki catches three less fish than Anna. How many fish did they catch in all?

_____

4. Every morning James makes a batch of biscuits. How many biscuits has James made after 5 mornings?

_____

5. Paul buys 3 boxes of pencils. His friend gives him 4 more pencils. How many pencils does Paul have?

_____

6. The students in a class are going to run a relay race. The class will be divided into three teams. How many students will be on each team?

_____

Solve each expression using the given value for the variable.

7. $△ = 3$

    $5 + △ =$ _____

8. $x = 9$

    $27 - x =$ _____

9. $x = 5$

    $9 × x =$ _____

10. $y = 10$

    $15 × y =$ _____

11. $p = 3$

    $6 × p + 7 =$ _____

12. $\boxed{*} = 8$

    $64 ÷ \boxed{*} =$ _____

Write an expression to solve each problem.

13. A herd of elephants lives in a grassland area. Half of the herd crosses a river and joins 3 elephants from another herd. Let △ stand for the number of elephants in the original herd. How many elephants are in the group now? _____

14. A baseball team shares the jobs of cleaning equipment. There are 4 different jobs. How many people do each type of job if there are 16 players? If there are 20 players? Use x to stand for the number of players and solve for each value of x. _____

CRCT Practice

Directions: Choose the best answer for each question. Circle the letter for the answer you have chosen.

1. Ms. Baxter's class is having a recycling drive. The class has 14 more pounds of newspapers than cans. Which expression shows how many pounds of newspapers they have collected?

   A. $14 - c$

   B. $c + 14$

   C. $c \times 14$

   D. $14 \div c$

2. What is the value of the expression

   $$5 \times y - 3 \text{ if } y = 5?$$

   A. 2

   B. 10

   C. 20

   D. 22

 3. If the expression $48 \div 4 + x = 15$ is true, what does x equal?

   A. 3

   B. 4

   C. 12

   D. 48

 4. Joanna planted 6 sunflower plants in her garden. Then she planted x more tulips than sunflowers. How many sunflowers and tulips did she plant in all?

   A. $x \times 6$

   B. $x + 6$

   C. $12 + x$

   D. $6 - x$

Lesson 43 Problem-Solving Strategy: Work Backwards

M4A1.b   Represent unknowns using symbols, such as △ and □.

M4A1.c   Write and evaluate mathematical expressions using symbols and different values.

M4P1.a   Solve non-routine word problems using the strategies of work backwards, use or make a table, and make an organized list as well as all strategies learned in previous grades.

You can work backwards and use related operations to solve problems.

Guided Instruction

Problem   Alex makes some brownies. He saves 10 of the brownies for his lunches at school. Then he eats 2 brownies. There are 12 brownies left. How many brownies did Alex make?

(U)nderstand the problem.

How many brownies did Alex save for lunches? _____

How many brownies did he eat? _____

How many brownies are left? _____

What do you need to find out? _____

_____

(M)ake a plan.

Start with what you know and work backwards. Write an expression that shows the events from the end to the beginning.

(S)olve the problem.

Start with the number of brownies left. Write and solve an expression to find the unknown number of brownies Alex made.

$$12 + 2 + \underline{\hspace{1cm}} = \underline{\hspace{1cm}}$$

Now let $\triangle$ stand for the unknown number of brownies. Write another expression for the problem.

$$\triangle - \underline{\hspace{1cm}} = \underline{\hspace{1cm}}$$

Use a related operation to work backwards and find the value of $\triangle$.

$$\underline{\hspace{1cm}} + \underline{\hspace{1cm}} = \triangle, \text{ so } \triangle = \underline{\hspace{1cm}}.$$

How many brownies did Alex make? _____

(C)heck your answer.

Rewrite each expression using 24 for $\triangle$.

$12 + 2 + 10 = 24$ and $24 - 12 = 12$.

Are the expressions true? _____

Apply the GPS

Work backwards to solve each problem. Show the expression and the variable that you used.

Work Space

1. Mark and his brother decide to plant pine trees. Mark plants 4 trees. His brother plants the rest of the trees. They plant 20 trees in all. How many trees did Mark's brother plant?

2. Tanya starts getting ready for a piano recital on Monday. Each day, she practices 10 minutes longer than on the last day. How long did she practice on Monday if she practiced for 45 minutes on Wednesday?

3. Max has $10 dollars saved up. He goes to the store and buys two comic books. If he has $6 left, how much did the books cost?

4. A pitcher holds 16 cups of water. After dinner, there are only 7 cups of water left in the pitcher. How much water was served with dinner?

5. A bag of cookies is divided among a class of students. Each student gets 3 cookies. There are 20 students in the class. How many cookies were in the bag?

6. A library is having a reading contest. John reads 4 more books than Tim. Lisa reads 2 more books than John. If the three students read 43 books altogether, how many books did Tim read?

7. Diana and Kelly both collect stamps. Kelly had 3 times as many stamps as Diana, but she gave away 5. Now Kelly has 88 stamps. How many stamps does Diana have?

CRCT Practice

**Directions: Choose the best answer for each question.
Circle the letter for the answer you have chosen.**

1. Elian opens a box of cookies and eats some. His friends eat 4 times as many cookies as he does. Now there are only 2 cookies left. If his friends ate 20 cookies, how many cookies were in the box?

    A. 32

    B. 17

    C. 27

    D. 25

2. What is the value of y in the expression $4 \times y = 48$?

    A. 48

    B. 44

    C. 18

    D. 12

3. What related operation would help you to find the value of $\square$?

     $+ 25 = 75$

    A. addition

    B. subtraction

    C. multiplication

    D. division

4. A school closes for 5 days because of a snow storm. That year, the students only go to school for 175 days. Which expression would tell you how many days are in a normal school year?

    A. $d = 180 - 175$

    B. $d = 180 + 175$

    C. $180 + d = 175$

    D. $175 + 5 = d$

Applying Concepts

Directions: Choose the best answer for each question. Circle the letter for the answer you have chosen.

1. What is the next number in this pattern?

    5, 10, 15, 20, 25, ?

   A. 50

   B. 40

   C. 30

   D. 20

2. What operation would make all of the number sentences true?

    $3 \boxed{} 3 = 9$

    $3 \boxed{} 4 = 12$

    $3 \boxed{} 5 = 15$

   A. +

   B. −

   C. ×

   D. ÷

3. Apply the following rule to the number 7.

   Rule: Subtract 3, then multiply the difference by 6.

   A. 42

   B. 24

   C. 21

   D. 7

4. What number is missing from the table?

	÷ 4
60	15
	9
28	7

   A. 30

   B. 42

   C. 36

   D. 46

5. What rule can you apply to each "In" number to get each "Out" number?

In	Out
5	10
6	12
7	14

   A. add 5

   B. multiply by 2

   C. multiply by 2 and add 1

   D. multiply by 2 and subtract 1

6. In which number sentence is 9 the missing number?

   A. $6 + \boxed{} = 17$

   B. $20 - \boxed{} = 9$

   C. $5 \times \boxed{} = 45$

   D. $42 \div 8 = \boxed{}$

Copying is illegal.   Measuring Up® to the Georgia Performance Standards

7. It takes 10 toothpicks to make the first row of the model below. Each row after that uses 7 more toothpicks. How many toothpicks in all are needed to make 3 rows?

A. 10

B. 17

C. 24

D. 30

8. A class of 20 students divides up into 5 teams. If Neil puts 2 of the teams together, how many students will be on the combined team?

A. 5

B. 8

C. 10

D. 20

9. Evaluate the expression for $\triangle = 3$.

$$\triangle + 8 \times 2$$

A. 19

B. 22

C. 24

D. 48

10. The first ride on the ferris wheel costs $5. Every ride after the first costs $1 less. How much money will it cost to ride the ferris wheel 3 times?

A. $10

B. $12

C. $15

D. $20

11. Complete the statement.

$$(12 + 2) \times 5 \div 2 = \text{?}$$

A. $5 + 3 \times 10$

B. $28 - 7 \times 10$

C. $54 \div 6 \times 3$

D. $2 + (5 \times 12) \div 2$

12. Which operation in the expression is done first?

$$36 \div 3 \times 4 + (18 - 8) \times 6$$

A. addition

B. subtraction

C. multiplication

D. division

13. Gregory is playing a computer game. If he scores 20 points in one game, his score is doubled. The table shows his points for 3 games. Which expression shows how many total points he won in the three games?

Game 1	Game 2	Game 3
18	15	20

A. $18 + 15 + (20 \times 2)$

B. $18 + (15 + 20)$

C. $18 + (15 \times 2) + 20$

D. $18 + 15 + 20$

14. Mrs. Spenser's class is collecting glass bottles and aluminum cans after a picnic. When they finish, they have 12 more pounds of glass than cans. Let c stand for the pounds of cans. How many pounds of glass have they collected?

A. $12 - c$

B. $c + 12$

C. $c \times 12$

D. $12 \div c$

15. Which expression describes the pattern of circles shown below?

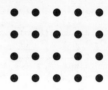

A. $5 + 5 + 5 + 5 + 5$

B. $4 + 4 + 4 + 4$

C. $4 + 5$

D. 4×5

16. Which symbol belongs in the ☐ to make a true number sentence?

$$12 \times 3 - 6 \boxed{} 2 \times (30 \times 1)$$

A. $=$

B. $\neq$

C. $<$

D. $>$

17. Sondra is tallying up the number of items her team collected on a treasure hunt. Four people each found 3 items. One person found 6 items. Another person lost one of the items that was found. Which expression shows how many items they collected altogether?

A. $4 \times 3 + 6 + 1$

B. $4 + 3 + 6 - 1$

C. $(4 \times 3) + 6 - 1$

D. $4 \times (3 + 6) - 1$

18. Which expression shows the rule for the table below?

64	8
32	4
24	3

A. $n + 8$

B. $n - 8$

C. $n \times 8$

D. $n \div 8$

19. If $5 + (\square \div 2) = 14$ is true, what is the value of $\square$?

A. 23

B. 18

C. 16

D. 7

20. On her vacation, Mara visits 4 cities. She buys a postcard for the same price in each city. If she uses all of her spending money on postcards, which expression shows how much spending money Mara had?

A. $p \times 4$

B. $p + 4$

C. $(4 \times p) + 4$

D. $4 - p$

21. Which operation would you use to help you solve the problem?

$$\boxed{} \div 9 = 9$$

A. $\times$

B. $\div$

C. $+$

D. $-$

22. Which is NOT a solution to the expression if the variable x is a multiple of 2?

$$3x + 1$$

A. 4

B. 7

C. 10

D. 19

23. Sean is on a road trip with his family. Each day, they drive 20 more miles than the day before. If they drove for 240 miles on Wednesday, how many miles did they drive on Sunday?

A. 220 miles

B. 200 miles

C. 180 miles

D. 160 miles

Chapter 7

Lesson 44 Estimate and Measure Length

Focus on GPS

M4M1.c	Compare one unit to another within a single system of measurement.
M4P1.b	Solve single and multi-step routine word problems related to all appropriate fourth grade math standards.

You can estimate and measure length in standard or metric units. Small units are best for shorter lengths. Large units are best for longer lengths.

Standard Units of Length	
inch (in.)	⊢————————⊣ 1 inch Smaller units are $\frac{1}{2}, \frac{1}{4}, \frac{1}{8}, \frac{1}{16}$ in.
foot (ft)	1 foot = 12 inches
yard (yd)	1 yard = 3 feet
mile (mi)	1 mile = 5,280 ft

Metric Units of Length	
centimeter (cm)	⊢——⊣ 1 centimeter **Millimeters** are shorter than centimeters. 10 mm = 1 cm
decimeter (dm)	1 decimeter = 10 cm
meter (m)	1 meter = 10 dm
kilometer (km)	1 kilometer = 1,000 m

Guided Instruction

Problem

Cal thinks the line below is 1 foot long. Is Cal correct? About how long is the line to the nearest half-inch? To the nearest cm?

————————————————————————

Use lengths you know to help you estimate and measure length.

Step 1   You know a ruler is 1 foot long. Is the length of the line greater than, equal to, or less than 1 rule? _____

Step 2   Compare the line to the inch and centimeter shown above.

About how many inches is it? _____ in.

About how many centimeters is it? _____ cm

Solution

Is the line 1 foot long? _____
About how long is the line in in. and cm? _____

Another Example

Which units would you use to measure the length of these items?

an ant	height of a door	distance between cities
Fraction of an in.	ft or _____	_____
_____	cm, dm, or _____	_____

Measuring Up® to the Georgia Performance Standards

Apply the GPS

Write each measurement. Use a ruler when you need to.

1. About how long is the rectangle to the nearest inch?

_____ inches

2. What is the length of the crayon to the nearest centimeter?

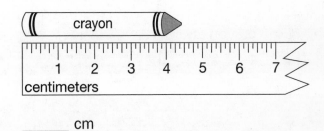

_____ cm

3. About how long is the needle to the nearest centimeter?

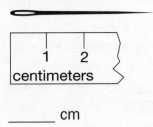

_____ cm

4. If the paper clip is 3 centimeters long, about how long is the stick?

_____ cm

Write the best unit for measuring the length of each: foot, inch, or mile.

5. the height of a building

_____

6. the length of a shoe

_____

Solve each problem. Explain your answer.

7. It takes Mia 20 minutes on a highway to drive from home to work. Which metric unit would be BEST to measure the distance from Mia's home to work? Explain. _____

_____

8. Tommy measures the height of a bookcase. He finds that it is 3 feet tall. Sela measures the height of another bookcase. She finds that it is 32 inches tall. Whose bookcase is taller? Explain. _____

_____

_____

9. James says the width of a fingertip is 1 meter long. Is he correct? Explain.

_____

_____

CRCT Practice **Directions: Choose the best answer for each question.**
Circle the letter for the answer you have chosen.

1. What is the length of the crayon to the nearest half-inch?

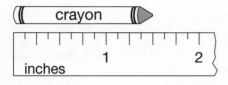

A. 2

B. $1\frac{1}{2}$

C. $1\frac{1}{4}$

D. 1

2. A square tile is 4 inches long on each side. About how long would a row of 9 of these tiles be?

A. 3 feet

B. 4 feet

C. 48 inches

D. 2 yards

3. Which of these would you NOT measure in meters?

A. height of a person

B. length of a room

C. height of a building

D. distance between cities

4. Jeff wants to measure the distance from his classroom door to the water fountain. It takes him 100 steps to walk from the door to the fountain. Which unit would be BEST for measuring this distance?

A. centimeter

B. kilometer

C. meter

D. millimeter

5. About how long is the paper clip to the nearest centimeter?

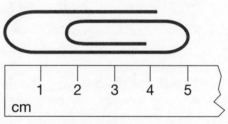

A. 3 centimeters

B. 4 centimeters

C. 5 centimeters

D. 6 centimeters

Lesson 45 Estimate and Measure Weight

M4M1.a	Use standard and metric units to measure the weight of objects.
M4M1.b	Know units used to measure weight (gram, kilogram, ounces, pounds, and tons).
M4M1.c	Compare one unit to another within a single system of measurement.
M4P2	Students will investigate, develop, and evaluate mathematical arguments.

You can estimate and measure weight in standard units. **Weight** is how heavy something is.

Standard Units of Weight		
ounce (oz)	AA	A small battery weighs about 1 ounce.
pound (lb)		Two baking potatoes weigh about 1 pound. 1 pound = 16 ounces
ton (ton)		A car weighs about 1 ton. 1 ton = 2,000 pounds

Guided Instruction

Problem A bag of plums weighs 2 pounds 8 ounces. If there are 10 plums in the bag, about how much does each plum weigh?

Step 1 One pound = 16 ounces. Which unit is greater, lb or oz? _____

If 10 plums weigh 2 lbs 8 oz, what unit should you use for the weight of 1 plum? _____

Step 2 Change pounds to ounces. Multiply the number of pounds times the number of ounces in 1 pound.

2 × 16 = _____ oz

Add the extra ounces to find the total weight of 10 plums.

_____ + 8 = _____ oz

Step 3 Now divide by 10 to estimate the weight of 1 plum.

_____ ÷ 10 = _____ oz

Solution About how much does each plum weigh? about _____

Apply the GPS   **Answer each question. Use a scale when you need to.**

1. Which could be the weight of a cat: 7 ounces, 7 pounds, or 7 tons?

_____

2. About how much does a tomato weigh: 6 ounces, 6 pounds, or 6 tons?

_____

3. About how much does a truck weigh: 5 ounces, 5 pounds, or 5 tons?

_____

4. Which could be the weight of a soup bowl: 1 ounce, 1 pound, or 1 ton?

_____

Write the best unit for measuring the weight of each: ounce, pound, or ton.

5. a big dog

_____

6. a ship

_____

7. eyeglasses

_____

Compare. Write >, <, or = in the ⬭.

8. 25 ounces ◯ 2 pounds

9. 2 tons ◯ 2,000 pounds

10. 3 pounds ◯ 38 ounces

11. 1 pound ◯ 20 ounces

Solve each problem. Explain your answer.

12. A potato weighs 9 ounces. About how many pounds would a bag of 9 potatoes weigh? Explain how you found your answer. _____

_____

13. Ali measures the weight of a melon. She finds that it weighs 3 lbs 2 oz. Ernesto measures the weight of another melon. He finds that it weighs 37 oz. Whose melon weighs more? Explain. _____

_____

_____

14. Ramon received a box that weighed 3 pounds. There were 8 softballs in the box. About how much did each softball weigh? Explain how you found your answer.

_____

_____

CRCT Practice

Directions: Choose the best answer for each question. Circle the letter for the answer you have chosen.

1. About how much does a bicycle weigh?

    A. 2 ounces

    B. 2 pounds

    C. 20 ounces

    D. 20 pounds

2. A baseball weighs 5 ounces. About how much would 6 baseballs weigh?

    A. 2 ounces

    B. 2 pounds

    C. 11 ounces

    D. 11 pounds

3. Adam needs to mail a small package so that it arrives the next day. Shipping company A charges $0.75 per ounce. Company B charges $15 per pound. Which of the following is TRUE?

    A. Company B charges less per ounce.

    B. Company A charges more per ounce.

    C. Company A charges less per pound.

    D. Company B charges less per pound.

4. Which of these could be the weight of a grapefruit?

    A. 8 ounces

    B. 8 days

    C. 8 feet

    D. 8 pounds

5. Mrs. Jansen received a box that weighed 4 pounds. The box held 9 drinking glasses that each weighed the same. About how much did each glass weigh?

    A. 5 ounces

    B. 7 ounces

    C. 5 pounds

    D. 13 pounds

Lesson 46 Estimate and Measure Mass

M4M1.a Use standard and metric units to measure the weight of objects.

M4M1.b Know units used to measure weight (gram, kilogram, ounces, pounds, and tons).

M4M1.c Compare one unit to another within a single system of measurement.

You can estimate and measure mass in metric units. **Mass** is how much matter something has.

Metric Units of Mass		
gram (g)		A large paper clip has a mass of about 1 gram. 1 gram = 1,000 milligrams
kilogram (kg)		A bunch of bananas has a mass of about 1 kilogram. 1 kilogram = 1,000 grams

Guided Instruction

Problem

Ann's bowling ball has a mass of about 6 kilograms. She used the ball to knock down 7 bowling pins. The mass of each pin is about 5,000 grams. Which has a greater mass, the bowling ball or the 7 pins?

Find each mass using the same units to compare.

Step 1 What is the mass of each pin? about _____ grams

Multiply by the number of pins to estimate the total mass.

_____ × 7 = _____ g

Step 2 Which unit is greater, kg or g? _____

How many grams make up 1 kilogram? _____

Multiply to find the mass of the bowling ball in grams.

_____ × 1,000 = _____ g

Step 3 Compare the two masses. Write the correct symbol.

35,000 g $\bigcirc$ 6,000 g

mass of 7 pins   mass of ball

Solution

Which has a greater mass, the bowling ball or the 7 pins?

_____

Apply the GPS

Answer each question. Use a balance or scale, if you wish.

1. Which could be the mass of a brick: 2 grams, 20 grams, or 2 kilograms?

_____

2. About how much is the mass of a pen: 5 grams, 5 kilograms, or 50 kilograms?

_____

3. About how much is the mass of a watermelon: 7 grams, 7 kilograms, or 70 kilograms?

_____

4. Which could be the mass of a paperback book: 9 grams, 90 grams, or 9 kilograms?

_____

Write the best unit for measuring the mass of each: gram or kilogram.

5. a television

_____

6. a crayon

_____

7. ruler

_____

Compare. Write >, <, or = in the ◯.

8. 400 grams ◯ 4 kilograms

9. 30 kilograms ◯ 3 grams

10. 6 kilograms ◯ 6,000 grams

11. 5,000 grams ◯ 1 kilogram

Solve each problem. Explain your answer.

12. A book has a mass of 110 grams. About how many kilograms would a carton of 9 of these books have? Explain how you found your answer. _____

_____

_____

13. Julio measures the mass of a cooking pot. He finds that it has a mass of 1 kilogram. Keira measures the mass of another cooking pot. She finds that it has a mass of 550 grams. Whose cooking pot has a greater mass? Explain.

_____

_____

14. Milt says the mass of his dog is about 10 kilograms. Could he be correct? Explain. _____

_____

_____

CRCT Practice

Directions: Choose the best answer for each question.
Circle the letter for the answer you have chosen.

1. About how much mass does a bag of flour have?

   A. 2 grams

   B. 2 kilograms

   C. 20 grams

   D. 20 kilograms

2. A grapefruit has a mass of 500 grams. How much mass would a bag of 8 grapefruits have?

   A. 80 grams

   B. 80 kilograms

   C. 4 grams

   D. 4 kilograms

3. Leon put a CD case on a balance to find its mass. Which of these could be the mass of the CD case?

   A. 60 days

   B. 60 feet

   C. 60 grams

   D. 60 kilograms

4. Mr. Lum received a box that had a mass of 3 kilograms. The 10 books in the box each had the same mass. What was the mass of each book?

   A. 30 grams

   B. 300 grams

   C. 30 kilograms

   D. 300 kilograms

5. Sally put a 5-gram weight on one side of a balance. Which of these objects probably does NOT weigh 5 grams?

   A. a softball

   B. a pencil

   C. a gumball

   D. a bottle cap

Lesson 47 Solve Problems Involving Measurement

M4G1 Students will define and identify the characteristics of geometric figures through examination and construction.
M4P5 Students will create and use pictures, manipulatives, models, and symbols to organize, record, and communicate mathematical ideas.

You can use measurement and information about figures to solve problems. The **perimeter** of a figure is the total distance around it. To find the perimeter of a polygon like a triangle or rectangle, add the lengths of all the sides.

Guided Instruction

Problem

Ed measured two walls of his room. What is the perimeter of his room?

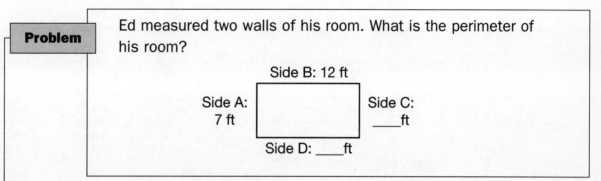

Side B: 12 ft
Side A: 7 ft
Side C: ____ft
Side D: ____ft

Use what you know about rectangles to find the perimeter.

Step 1 Find the length of each side.

Side	A	B	C	D
Length	7 ft	12 ft	_____	_____

Step 2 Add the lengths of the sides to find the perimeter.

_____ + _____ + _____ + _____ = _____ feet

The perimeter of Ed's room is _____ feet.

Solution What is the perimeter of Ed's room? _____ feet

Another Example

Nan wants to build a fence around her backyard. How many meters of fencing will she need? Hint: Side C + Side E = Side A

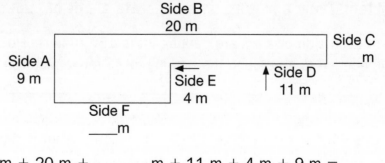

Side B
20 m
Side A
9 m
Side C
____m
Side E
4 m
Side D
11 m
Side F
____m

9 m + 20 m + _____ m + 11 m + 4 m + 9 m = _____ m

Apply the GPS Solve each problem.

1. What is the perimeter of the garden?

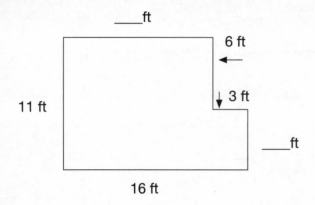

____ft

6 ft

11 ft

3 ft

____ft

16 ft

_____

2. What is the perimeter of the shape?

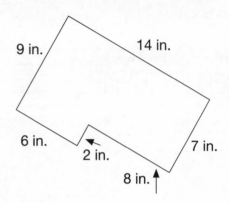

9 in.

14 in.

6 in.

2 in.

7 in.

8 in.

_____

3. What is the perimeter of the frame?

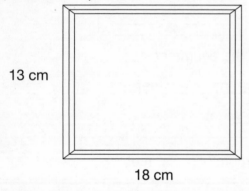

13 cm

18 cm

_____

4. What is the perimeter of the figure?

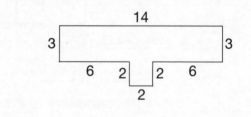

14

3

3

6   2   2   6

2

_____

Solve each problem. Draw a picture on a separate sheet of paper.

5. The length of each side of a square parking lot is 150 meters. How many meters of fencing is needed to go around the parking lot? Draw a picture. _____

_____

6. Eva sews 3 feet 8 inches of lace onto the four edges of a rectangular tablecloth. One edge of the tablecloth is 9 inches long. What is the length in inches of the other three edges? Draw a picture. _____

_____

Measuring Up® to the Georgia Performance Standards

CRCT Practice

Directions: Choose the best answer for each question.

Circle the letter for the answer you have chosen.

 1. This is a picture of Sam's yard. What is the perimeter of the yard?

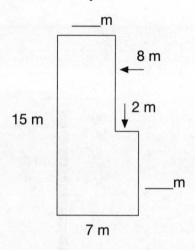

____m

8 m

2 m

15 m

____m

7 m

A. 34 meters

B. 32 meters

C. 42 meters

D. 44 meters

2. What is the perimeter of the figure?

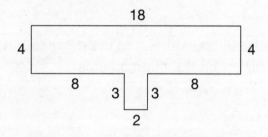

18

4   4

8   8

3   3

2

A. 50 units

B. 50 square units

C. 40 units

D. 40 square units

3. Lex uses 4 feet 2 inches of wood to make the four sides of a rectangular picture frame. One side of the frame is 12 inches long. What is the length, of the other side of the frame?

A. 9 inches

B. 13 inches

C. 18 inches

D. 26 inches

 4. Wendy drew a picture of her room. What is the perimeter of her room?

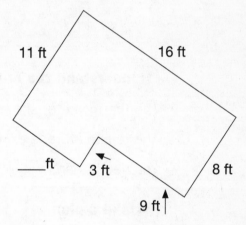

11 ft   16 ft

____ft   3 ft   8 ft

9 ft

A. 44 feet

B. 47 feet

C. 54 feet

D. 64 feet

Focus on GPS

Lesson 48 **Problem-Solving Strategy: Use Information from Pictures**

M4N7.a   Describe situations in which the four operations may be used and the relationships among them.
M4P5   Students will create and use pictures, manipulatives, models, and symbols to organize, record, and communicate mathematical ideas.

You can use information from pictures to solve problems. **Temperature** measures how hot or cold something is. The customary unit for temperature is **degrees Fahrenheit (°F)**. **Elapsed time** is the amount of time that passes from one time to another.

Guided Instruction

Problem

The thermometer shows the temperature outside on Monday morning. If the temperature is expected to rise 15 degrees to be warmer by this afternoon, what will the temperature in the afternoon be?

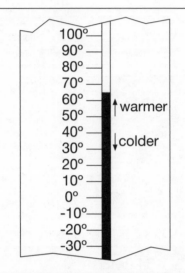

Understand the problem.

The thermometer shows the _____ on Monday morning.

The temperature is expected to _____ degrees by this afternoon.

You need to find _____

Make a plan.

Use information from the picture. Read the temperature. Add the degrees it will rise. If the temperature **rises**, find a number higher on the thermometer.

Solve the problem.

Read the temperature on the thermometer. The temperature is _____ °F.

Add: 65 + 15 = _____

What will the temperature in the afternoon be? _____ °F

Check your answer.

Subtract to check. 80 − 15 = _____ °F.

Apply the GPS

Solve each problem.

1. The temperature on Monday was 12° colder than Sunday. What was the temperature on Monday?

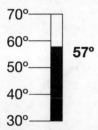

70°
60°
50°
40°
30°

57°

Sunday's Temperature

_____ °F

2. The class play is on the third Thursday in January. What is the date of the class play?

JANUARY						
Sun	Mon	Tue	Wed	Thu	Fri	Sat
		1	2	3	4	5
6	7	8	9	10	11	12
13	14	15	16	17	18	19
20	21	22	23	24	25	26
27	28	29	30	31		

_____

3. If it takes Troy 40 minutes to walk from home to work, what is the latest time he can leave to get to work by 8:30 A.M.?

Time at work

_____ A.M.

4. The clock shows when Elsa started to read a book. She finished 2 hours and 25 minutes later. At what time did Elsa finish reading?

_____

Answer each question. Use the picture for questions 5–6.

5. What temperature does the thermometer show?

_____

6. If the temperature is expected to be 11° cooler later on, what will the temperature be later? Explain your answer. _____

_____

_____

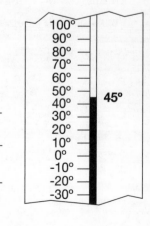

100°
90°
80°
70°
60°
50°
40°
30°
20°
10°
0°
-10°
-20°
-30°

45°

CRCT Practice

Directions: Choose the best answer for each question.
Circle the letter for the answer you have chosen.

Use the thermometer below for questions 1 and 2.

1. Read the temperature for Friday. The temperature on Thursday was 5° colder than on Friday. What was the temperature on Thursday?

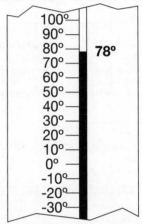

Friday Morning's Temperature

   A.   28°F

   B.   72°F

   C.   73°F

   D.   83°F

2. If the temperature is expected to rise 10 degrees on Friday afternoon, what will the afternoon temperature be?

   A.   89°F

   B.   88°F

   C.   79°F

   D.   68°F

 3. Deana started her science project at 4:50. If she finished it in 1 hour and 15 minutes, when did Deana finish?

Start Time

   A.   5:50 P.M.

   B.   6:05 P.M.

   C.   6:10 P.M.

   D.   6:15 P.M.

 4. Vera started swim lessons in May. She had a lesson every Monday, Friday, and Saturday. If she had 9 swim lessons in May, what day did she start?

MAY						
Sun	Mon	Tue	Wed	Thu	Fri	Sat
			1	2	3	4
5	6	7	8	9	10	11
12	13	14	15	16	17	18
19	20	21	22	23	24	25
26	27	28	29	30	31	

   A.   May 10

   B.   May 11

   C.   May 12

   D.   May 13

Applying Concepts

Directions: Choose the best answer for each question.
Circle the letter for the answer you have chosen.

1. Which unit would be used to measure the height of a ladder?

   A. centimeter

   B. gram

   C. meter

   D. ton

2. The doctor measured the weight of Kento's baby brother, who is almost 1 year old. Which of these could be the weight of Kento's baby brother?

   A. 18 days

   B. 18 degrees

   C. 18 feet

   D. 18 pounds

3. Look at the picture frame below.

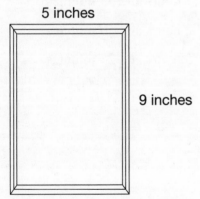

   5 inches

   9 inches

   What is the perimeter of the frame?

   A. 14 inches

   B. 28 inches

   C. 45 inches

   D. 59 inches

4. About how much mass does a bicycle have?

   A. 12 ounces

   B. 2 pounds

   C. 2 grams

   D. 12 kilograms

5. The thermometer shows the temperature for Tuesday. The temperature on Monday was 15° warmer than on Tuesday. What was the temperature on Monday?

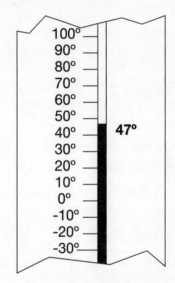

   Tuesday's Temperature

   A. 35°F

   B. 52°F

   C. 55°F

   D. 62°F

6. About how long is the rectangle?

|—————| 1 centimeter

A. 1 centimeter

B. 2 centimeters

C. 4 centimeters

D. 5 centimeters

7. A volleyball weighs 9 ounces. About how much would a bag of 4 volleyballs weigh?

A. 2 pounds

B. 3 pounds

C. 13 ounces

D. 13 kilograms

8. Edna put a coin on a scale to find its mass. Which of these could be the mass of the coin?

A. 2 days

B. 2 feet

C. 2 grams

D. 2 kilograms

9. This is a picture of Tran's room. What is the perimeter of his room?

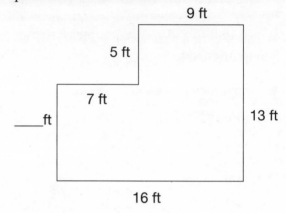

A. 48 ft

B. 50 ft

C. 58 ft

D. 63 ft

10. If Salma started her book report at 3:35 P.M. and finished it at 5:50 P.M., how long did it take Salma to do her book report?

A. 2 hours and 15 minutes

B. 2 hours and 35 minutes

C. 2 hours and 50 minutes

D. 5 hours and 25 minutes

11. Ali wants to measure the distance from his home to the baseball stadium. It takes him 30 minutes on a highway to get to the stadium by car. Which unit would be BEST for measuring the distance from Ali's home to the stadium?

    A. centimeter

    B. kilometer

    C. meter

    D. millimeter

12. About how much does a peach weigh?

    A. 5 grams

    B. 5 kilograms

    C. 5 ounces

    D. 5 pounds

13. A tomato has a mass of 400 grams. About how much mass would a container of 5 tomatoes have?

    A. 2 kilograms

    B. 4 ounces

    C. 4 pounds

    D. 405 grams

14. A ribbon measures 7 inches long. What would be the total length of 3 of these ribbons?

    A. 1 foot, 5 inches

    B. 1 foot, 9 inches

    C. 2 feet, 1 inch

    D. 3 feet, 1 inch

15. The length of each side of a square playground is 18 meters. How many meters of fencing are needed to go around the playground?

    A. 18 meters

    B. 36 meters

    C. 72 meters

    D. 324 meters

16. What label is missing from the chart?

	Temperature
9:00 A.M.	67°
11:00 A.M.	70°
1:00 P.M.	74°
3:00 P.M.	80°
5:00 P.M.	75°
7:00 P.M.	71°
9:00 P.M.	60°

    A. Day

    B. Hour

    C. Month

    D. Year

17. A book weighs 1 pound and 6 ounces. How many ounces does the book weigh?

    A. 16 ounces

    B. 18 ounces

    C. 21 ounces

    D. 22 ounces

18. About how much mass does a pencil have?

    A. 5 grams

    B. 5 kilograms

    C. 15 pounds

    D. 150 ounces

19. What is the perimeter of the figure below?

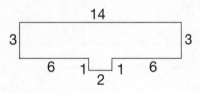

    A. 36 units

    B. 36 sq. units

    C. 34 units

    D. 34 sq. units

20. It takes Andy 25 minutes to walk from home to the library. What is the latest time he can leave home to get to the library by the time shown below?

    A. 1:20 P.M.

    B. 1:25 P.M.

    C. 1:50 P.M.

    D. 2:15 P.M.

21. Look at the pencil below. Use the ruler to estimate the length of the pencil to the nearest inch.

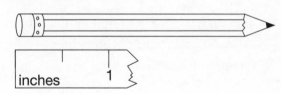

    A. 1 inch

    B. 2 inches

    C. 3 inches

    D. 4 inches

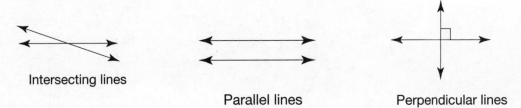

Chapter 8

Lesson 49 Identify Parallel and Perpendicular Lines

Focus on GPS

M4G1.b Describe parallel and perpendicular lines in plane geometric figures.

M4P3 Students will use the language of mathematics to express ideas precisely.

M4P5 Students will create and use pictures, manipulatives, models, and symbols to organize, record, and ommunicate mathematical ideas.

A **line** is a straight path that extends in two directions.

A **line segment** is part of a line with two endpoints.

Intersecting lines meet or intersect at one point.

Parallel lines never intersect and are the same distance apart everywhere.

Perpendicular lines intersect and form square corners.

Intersecting lines   Parallel lines   Perpendicular lines

Guided Instruction

Problem Which streets on the map are parallel to Franklin Drive? Which streets are perpendicular to Richmond Street?

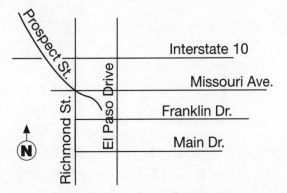

Step 1 Streets that never meet are parallel. Which streets are parallel to Franklin Drive? _____

Step 2 Streets that form square corners are perpendicular. Which streets are perpendicular to Richmond Street? _____

_____

Which streets are parallel to Franklin Drive?

Solution

_____

Which streets are perpendicular to Richmond Street?

_____

Apply the GPS

Write intersecting, perpendicular, or parallel for each pair of lines.

1.
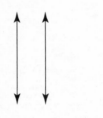

_____

2.

_____

3.
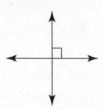

_____

4.

_____

5.

_____

6.
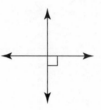

_____

Answer each question.

7. What type of lines are the heavy black lines on the flag? Explain your answer.

_____

_____

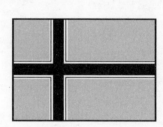

Flag of Norway

8. Ashley is driving down Oak Street. She knows that her best friend lives on Elm Street. Elm Street is parallel to Oak Street. If Ashley stays on Oak Street, will the road ever intersect with Elm Street? Why or why not?

_____

9. Brian is making a map. He draws Main Street going from the east to the west. Then he draws First Street, Third Street, and Fifth Street perpendicular to Main Street. Draw Brian's map below. Label each street.

 Measuring Up® to the Georgia Performance Standards

CRCT Practice

Directions: Choose the best answer for each question.
Circle the letter for the answer you have chosen.

1. Which of these is an example of perpendicular lines?

   A.

   B.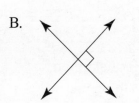

   C.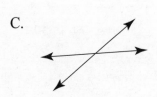

   D.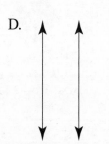

2. Which symbol or letter is made from perpendicular lines?

   A. +

   B. X

   C. =

   D. V

3. Which set of line segments is neither parallel nor perpendicular?

   A.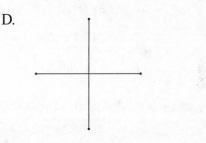

   B.

   C.

   D.

4. Molly is giving directions from her house to the grocery store. She tells her friend to turn right from Orchid Street to Lake Street. What must be true about Orchid Street and Lake Street?

   A. The streets are parallel.

   B. The streets are not perpendicular.

   C. The streets do not intersect.

   D. The streets intersect.

Focus on GPS

Lesson 50 Measure Angles

| **M4M2.a** | Use tools, such as a protractor or angle ruler, and other methods such as paper folding, drawing a diagonal in a square, to measure angles. |
| **M4P5** | Students will create and use pictures, manipulatives, models, and symbols to organize, record, and communicate mathematical ideas. |

A **ray** is a part of a line with one endpoint.

When two rays share an endpoint, they form an **angle**. The shared endpoint is called the **vertex**.

The size of an angle is measured in **degrees**. To measure and draw angles, you can use a **protractor**. This protractor shows a 90-degree or 90° angle.

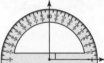

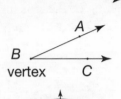

Guided Instruction

| **Problem** | Nell is hiking along a straight path to the east. Her field map shows a campsite nearby. How many degrees north should Nell turn to find the campsite? |

Step 1 Use the straightedge of your protractor to draw two rays. Draw a ray from Nell to the east end of the path. Then draw a ray from Nell to the campsite.

What is the vertex of the angle you drew?

_____

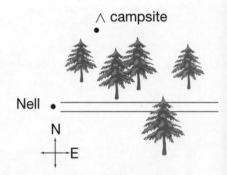

Step 2 Place the protractor over the bottom ray of the angle, so the center hole is over the vertex. Hint: Look at the protractor and 90° angle above. What is the measure of the angle you drew? _____

| **Solution** | How many degrees north should Nell turn? _____ |

Another Example

You can find out if an angle is a 90° angle without using a protractor.

Fold a piece of paper in half.

Fold the paper in half in the other direction.

Unfold the paper. Compare your angle to a folded angle.

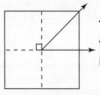

The angles are not the same, so this is not a right angle.

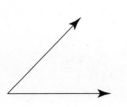

Apply the GPS

Use a protractor to measure each angle.

1.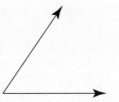
_____

2.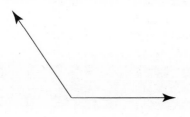
_____

3.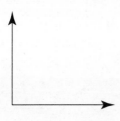
_____

4.
_____

5.
_____

6.
_____

Use your protractor to draw each angle.

7. Draw an angle that measures 140°. Label the vertex B.

8. Draw an angle that measures 30°. Label the vertex Q.

Answer each question.

9. Lines A and B are perpendicular. How many angles are formed? _____

What is the measurement of each angle? _____

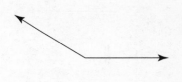

10. Draw two intersecting lines on another sheet. Measure and label each of the angles formed. What is the sum of the measurements of the angles? _____

CRCT Practice   **Choose the best answer for each question.**

Circle the letter for the answer you have chosen.

1. Which of these angles measures less than 90°?

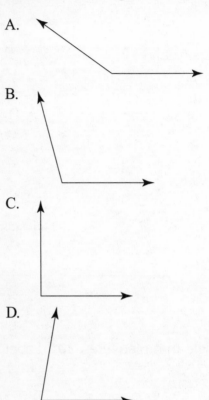

A.

B.

C.

D.

2. What is the measure of an angle that is formed by two perpendicular lines?

A. 30°

B. 45°

C. 60°

D. 90°

3. Which method could you use to make an angle that measures 45°?

A. Fold a piece of paper in half.

B. Fold a piece of paper in half and then fold it in half again.

C. Fold a square piece of paper in half along the diagonal line between opposite corners.

D. Cut a piece of paper in half and draw a line on one half.

4. Use a protractor to find the measure of the angle shown below.

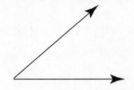

A. 40°

B. 45°

C. 50°

D. 55°

Lesson 51 Classify Angles and Triangles

M4G1.a   Examine and compare angles in order to classify and identify triangles by their angles.
M4P3   Students will use the language of mathematics to express ideas precisely.
M4P5   Students will create and use pictures, manipulatives, models, and symbols to organize, record, and communicate mathematical ideas.

You can use angle measurements to name different angles and triangles.

A **right angle** measures exactly 90°.

An **acute angle** measures less than 90°.

An **obtuse angle** measures more than 90°.

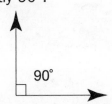
90°

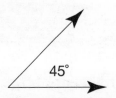
45°

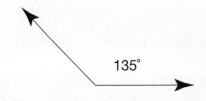
135°

A **right triangle** has one right angle.

An **acute triangle** has three acute angles.

An **obtuse triangle** has one obtuse angle.

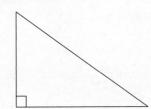

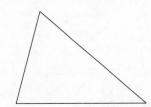

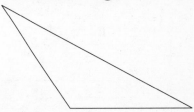

Guided Instruction

Problem   Jason is looking at the angles formed by the hands on a clock. What types of angles are formed at 8:50, 9:00, and 9:10?

Step 1   Shade the angles between the hands of the clocks. Shade the whole area from the vertex of the angle to the edge of the clock face.

Step 2   Identify the angles you shaded.

Which time shows a right angle? _____

Which time shows an acute angle? _____

Which time shows an obtuse angle? _____

Solution
What angle is formed at 8:50? _____ angle

What angle is formed at 9:00? _____ angle

What angle is formed at 9:10? _____ angle

Identify each angle as acute, right, or obtuse.

1.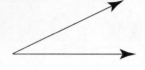

_____

2.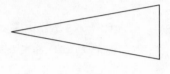

_____

3.

_____

Identify each triangle as acute, right, or obtuse.

4.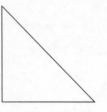

_____

5.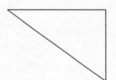

_____

6.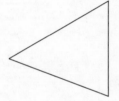

_____

7.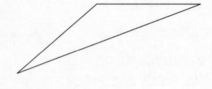

_____

8.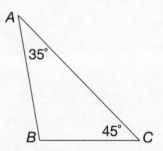

_____

9.

_____

Use the figure to answer questions 10–12.

10. What kind of angles are in triangle *ABC*?

angle *A* _____

angle *B* _____

angle *C* _____

11. What kind of triangle is triangle *ABC*?

_____

12. The sum of the three angle measures in a triangle always equals 180°. Use this fact to find the missing angle measure in the triangle *ABC*. Explain your answer.

_____

_____

CRCT Practice Directions: Choose the best answer for each question.
Circle the letter for the answer you have chosen.

1. Which of these is an example of an acute triangle?

    A.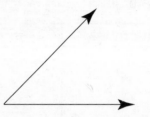

    B.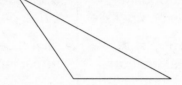

    C.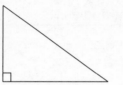

    D.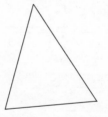

2. Which describes the angle shown below?

    A. obtuse angle

    B. acute angle

    C. right angle

    D. straight line

3. Which triangle has one angle that is greater than 90°?

    A.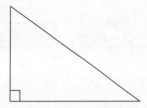

    B.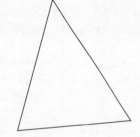

    C.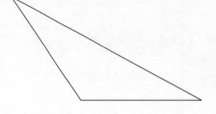

    D.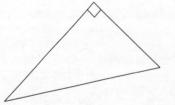

4. Which of the following statements is true?

    A. A right triangle has one obtuse angle.

    B. A right triangle has only one right angle.

    C. An acute triangle has only one acute angle.

    D. An obtuse triangle has more than one obtuse angle.

M4G1.c	Examine and classify quadrilaterals (including parallelograms, squares, rectangles, trapezoids, and rhombi).
M4G1.d	Compare and contrast the relationships among quadrilaterals.
M4P3	Students will use the language of mathematics to express ideas precisely.
M4P5	Students will create and use pictures, manipulatives, models, and symbols to organize, record, and communicate mathematical ideas.

You can use sides and angles to name different kinds of quadrilaterals. A **quadrilateral** is a closed shape made from four line segments called **sides**. Look at the names and features of some special quadrilaterals.

Trapezoid	Parallelogram	Rhombus	Rectangle	Square
• 1 pair of parallel sides	• opposite sides parallel • opposite sides equal length	• opposite sides parallel • all 4 sides equal length	• opposite sides parallel • opposite sides equal length • 4 right angles	• opposite sides parallel • all 4 sides equal length • 4 right angles

Guided Instruction

Problem

Eduardo has a quadrilateral that he wants to classify. Which names can he use to describe the quadrilateral? Which name BEST describes it?

Step 1 How many pairs of sides are parallel? _____

How many pairs of equal sides are there? _____

Are all sides the same length? _____

How many angles are right angles? _____

Step 2 List two quadrilaterals with opposite sides that are both parallel and equal length. _____

Which of these also describes the angles of this quadrilateral?

_____

Solution

Which names can he use to describe the quadrilateral?

_____ Which best describes it?

_____

Measuring Up® to the Georgia Performance Standards

Apply the GPS

Circle the correct or best name for each quadrilateral.

1.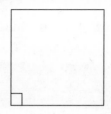

Rhombus   Square

2.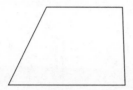

Trapezoid   Parallelogram

3.

Parallelogram   Rhombus

Identify each quadrilateral. Write the best name for each.

4.

_____

5.

_____

6.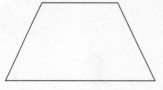

_____

7.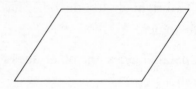

_____

8.

_____

9.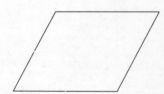

_____

Answer each question.

10. Look at the quadrilateral. Draw arrows (◄──►) between each set of parallel lines. Mark sides of equal length with an X. Circle any right angles. What is the best name for the quadrilateral?

_____

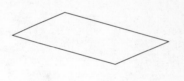

11. Is this quadrilateral a special quadrilateral? Explain.

_____

_____

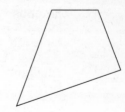

12. Which quadrilaterals have perpendicular sides? Explain.

_____

_____

CRCT Practice

Directions: Choose the best answer for each question.
Circle the letter for the answer you have chosen.

1. Which of these quadrilaterals is NOT a parallelogram?

A.

B.

C.

D.

2. What kind of quadrilateral is shown below?

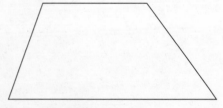

A. parallelogram

B. rhombus

C. trapezoid

D. rectangle

3. Which is NOT another name you could use to describe a square?

A. parallelogram

B. rectangle

C. rhombus

D. trapezoid

4. What is the difference between a rhombus and a parallelogram?

A. One has opposite sides of equal length, the other has all four sides the same length.

B. One has two right angles, the other has four right angles.

C. One has parallel sides, the other does not have parallel sides.

D. One has one set of parallel sides, the other has two sets of parallel sides.

Measuring Up® to the Georgia Performance Standards

Lesson 53 Describe and Compare Rectangular Prisms

M4G2.a Compare and contrast a cube and a rectangular prism in terms of the number and shape of their faces, edges, and vertices.

M4G2.b Describe parallel and perpendicular lines and planes in connection with the rectangular prism.

M4G2.c Construct/collect models for solid geometric figures (cube, prisms, cylinder, etc.).

M4P5 Students will create and use pictures, manipulatives, models, and symbols to organize, record, and communicate mathematical ideas.

A **prism** is a 3-dimensional or solid figure. A **rectangular prism** is made up of 6 sides called **faces** that are all rectangles. A **cube** is a special rectangular prism made up of 6 square faces that are the same size.

Rectangular Prism

vertex

edge

face

An **edge** is a line segment where 2 faces meet.

A **vertex** (plural: vertices) is a point where 3 or more edges meet.

Guided Instruction

Problem

Alice made a cardboard box to hold a gift. How many faces, edges, and vertices does her box have? Is the box a cube?

How many faces or sides does the box have? _____

What is the shape of each face? _____

How many edges does the box have? _____

How many vertices does the box have? _____

Solution

How many faces, edges, and vertices does her box have? _____ faces, _____ edges, and _____ vertices. Is the box a cube? _____

Another Example

Look at the cardboard Alice used to make a different box. Is the box a rectangular prism or a cube?

_____

Name a pair of faces that are parallel and have parallel edges. _____

A

B

E   C   F

D

_____

Name a pair of faces that are perpendicular and have perpendicular edges. _____

_____

Identify each figure as a rectangular prism or a cube

1.

_____

2.

_____

3.

_____

Complete the table below.

Prism	Shape of Faces	Number of Faces	Number of Edges	Number of Vertices
4.	_____	_____ faces	_____ edges	_____ vertices
5.	_____	_____ faces	_____ edges	_____ vertices

Answer each question.

6. Label an example of a face, a vertex, and an edge on the figure.

7. Color two parallel faces on the prism. Then draw thick lines on two parallel edges.

8. Color two perpendicular faces on the prism. Then draw thick lines on two perpendicular edges.

9. Is the figure a cube? Explain why or why not.

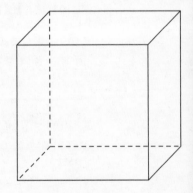

_____

_____

 Measuring Up® to the Georgia Performance Standards

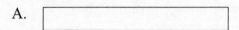

CRCT Practice   Directions: Choose the best answer for each question.
Circle the letter for the answer you have chosen.

1. Which of these quadrilaterals could be used to make a cube?

   A.

   B.

   C.

   D.

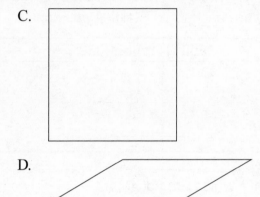

2. Which statement is NOT true of the prism shown below?

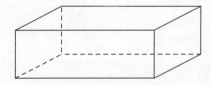

   A. It has fewer faces than edges.

   B. It has more vertices than edges.

   C. It has sets of perpendicular lines.

   D. It has sets of parallel lines.

3. A solid figure has parallel faces and perpendicular faces. Two parallel faces have edges that are shorter than the edges for the other faces. What kind of figure could this be?

   A. square

   B. cube

   C. rectangle

   D. rectangular prism

 4. Carol has a rectangular prism. If she cuts the prism in half as shown, what shapes is she left with?

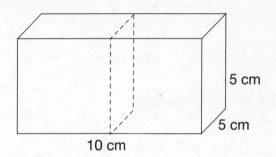

5 cm

5 cm

10 cm

   A. two cubes

   B. one cube and one rectangular prism

   C. two rectangular prisms

   D. one square and one rectangle

Lesson 54 Use Visual Thinking to Solve Problems

M4G1.c	Examine and classify quadrilaterals (including parallelograms, squares, rectangles, trapezoids, and rhombi).
M4M2.b	Understand the meaning and measure of a half rotation (180 degrees) and a full rotation (360 degrees).
M4P5	Students will create and use pictures, manipulatives, models, and symbols to organize, record, and communicate mathematical ideas.

You can compare the size and shape of figures. **Similar** figures have the same shape but can be different sizes. **Congruent** figures have the same shape and size. A figure has **symmetry** if it can be folded on a line to make two congruent parts. Some symmetrical figures have more than one **line of symmetry.**

Similar Figures	Congruent Figures	Symmetrical Figures

You can rotate or turn a figure without changing its shape or size. A **rotation** moves a figure around a point. A **full rotation** moves a figure back to its starting position.

Half Rotation (180°)	Full Rotation (360°)

Guided Instruction

Problem 1

Which of these figures are similar? Which are congruent?

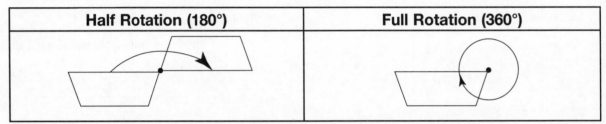

Step 1 Look at the two squares. They are the same shape.

Are they the same size? _____

The squares are not congruent. Are they similar? _____

Step 2 Are the parallelograms the same shape? _____

Are they the same size? _____

Are they congruent? _____ Are they similar? _____

Step 3 Are the triangles the same shape? _____

Are they the same size? _____

Are they congruent? _____ Are they similar? _____

Solution

Which figures are similar? _____

Which are congruent? _____

Guided Instruction

Problem 2

Adam needs to cut out letters to spell GEORGIA on a poster. He is going to fold a piece of paper in half and cut out half of the letter on the fold. When he unfolds the paper, he will have a symmetrical letter. Which letters can Adam make using this method?

Use the dashed lines to check each letter for symmetry. Compare the top and bottom halves and the left and right halves of each letter.

Which letters have symmetry? _____

Which letters do not have symmetry? _____

Solution

Which letters can Adam make using the lines of symmetry?

_____

Another Problem

What kind of rotation is shown by figures A and B?
Are the figures congruent?

Trace figure A on a piece of paper. Turn the paper so figure A covers figure B.

What kind of rotation did you use? _____

Are the figures congruent? Explain.

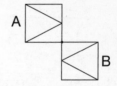

_____

_____

Apply the GPS

Write *congruent*, *similar*, or *neither* for each pair of figures.

1.

_____

2.

_____

3.

_____

4.

_____

5.

_____

6.

_____

Write *true* or *false* to tell if each figure is symmetrical. Draw the lines of symmetry.

7.

_____

8.

_____

9.

_____

Answer each question.

10. Draw a half rotation of the figure. How many degrees did you rotate the figure? _____

What would the figure look like after a full rotation? Explain. _____

_____

11. How can a pair of figures be similar, but not congruent?

_____

CRCT Practice

Directions: Choose the best answer for each question. Circle the letter for the answer you have chosen.

1. Which pair of figures is congruent?

   A.

   B.

   C.

   D.

   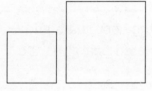

   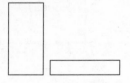

2. Gina wants to find out if a shape has symmetry. She folds the shape along a line. What is she checking for?

   A. congruent halves

   B. similar halves

   C. triangles

   D. quadrilaterals

3. Two squares are drawn on a sheet of paper. What additional information do you need to tell if they are congruent or similar?

   A. their colors

   B. the number of vertices

   C. the number of sides

   D. their sizes

4. Which is true of the figures shown below?

   A. They are congruent.

   B. They are similar.

   C. They show a half rotation.

   D. They show a full rotation.

Lesson 55 Locate and Graph Ordered Pairs

M4G3.a	Understand and apply ordered pairs in the first quadrant of the coordinate system.
M4G3.b	Locate a point in the first quadrant in the coordinate plane and name the ordered pair.
M4G3.c	Graph ordered pairs in the first quadrant.
M4P3	Students will use the language of mathematics to express ideas precisely.

You can use ordered pairs to find, name, or plot points on a coordinate grid.

An **ordered pair** is a pair of numbers that gives the location of a point. The first number tells how many units to move to the right of 0. The second number tells how many units to move up. The ordered pair (3, 2) locates the point shown on this grid.

Guided Instruction

Problem

Lily made a map of her neighborhood on the coordinate grid below. What is located at (4, 7)? What ordered pair gives the location of her friend Stella's house?

Step 1 Look at the first number in the ordered pair (4, 7).

Move _____ units to the right of 0.

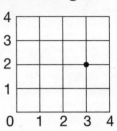

Step 2 Look at the second number in the ordered pair.

Move _____ units up.

What is located at the point (4, 7)? _____

Step 3 Now find the point for Stella's house.

Look down the line to the numbers on the bottom of the grid.

Stella's house is _____ units to the right of 0.

Step 4 Look at the numbers on the left side of the grid.

Stella's house is _____ units up from the bottom.

Write the ordered pair. _____

Solution

What is located at (4, 7)? _____ What is the ordered pair for Stella's house? _____

Another Problem

Lily's house is located at (2, 9). On the map grid above, draw the point (2, 9) and label it Lily's House.

Which is closer to Lily's house, the school or John's house?

_____

_____

 Measuring Up® to the Georgia Performance Standards

Apply the GPS

Write the letter for each point on the coordinate grid.

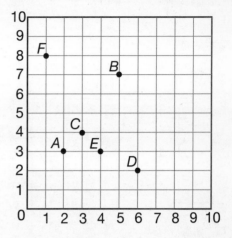

1. (5, 7)

_____

2. (1, 8)

_____

3. (3, 4)

_____

4. (6, 2)

_____

5. (4, 3)

_____

6. (2, 3)

_____

Write the ordered pair for each lettered point on the coordinate grid.

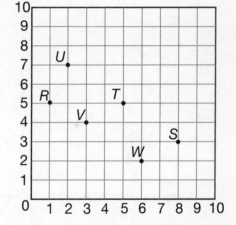

7. R

_____

8. S

_____

9. T

_____

10. U

_____

11. V

_____

12. W

_____

Use the coordinate grid for questions 13 and 14.

13. Graph and connect the three points to draw a figure.

(3, 4), (9, 6), (4, 9)

What kind of figure did you draw? _____

14. What would happen if you plotted and connected the point (9, 4) instead of (4, 9)? _____

_____

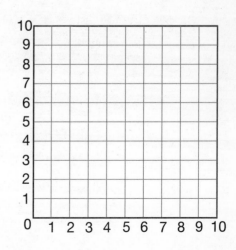

CRCT Practice **Directions: Choose the best answer for each question.**
Circle the letter for the answer you have chosen.

Use the coordinate grid to answer questions 1 and 2.

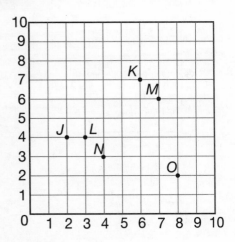

1. Which point is at (7, 6)?

    A. point *K*

    B. point *L*

    C. point *M*

    D. point *N*

2. What is the ordered pair at point *O*?

    A. (2, 8)

    B. (8, 2)

    C. (2, 4)

    D. (4, 6)

3. There are two points on a grid. Point *A* is at (2, 3). Point *C* is four units to the right of point *A* and three units higher on the grid. What is the ordered pair for point *C*?

    A. (2, 3)

    B. (3, 2)

    C. (7, 5)

    D. (6, 6)

4. Which ordered pair gives a point that is located on the bottom line of a grid?

    A. (6, 0)

    B. (0, 3)

    C. (0, 5)

    D. (10, 10)

5. A point located at (4, 9) is moved down two units. Which ordered pair gives the new location of the point?

    A. (2, 7)

    B. (2, 9)

    C. (4, 7)

    D. (4, 11)

Lesson 56 Problem-Solving Strategy: Use Logic

M4G1.d	Compare and contrast the relationships among quadrilaterals.
M4P2	Students will investigate, develop, and evaluate mathematical arguments.
M4P3	Students will use the language of mathematics to express ideas precisely.

Guided Instruction

Problem Marsha is trying to prove to a friend that squares are also rectangles. How can she use logic to explain this relationship?

Understand the problem.

What are the features of a rectangle? _____

_____

What are the features of a square? _____

_____

Make a plan.

Use what you know about squares and rectangles to model their relationship. Make a Venn diagram to show how they are alike and different.

Solve the problem.

Make a Venn diagram like the one below.

square — all sides are congruent | 4 sides, 4 vertexes, 4 right angles, parallel lines, perpendicular lines — rectangle

What is the one feature that makes a rectangle a square?

_____

How can Marsha explain the relationship between squares and rectangles?

_____

_____

Check your answer.

Test your model by looking at examples. Check the features of each example against your Venn diagram.

Apply the GPS

Use Venn diagrams to answer the questions. Explain your answers.

Work Space

1. Can a square be a rhombus?

square   rhombus

_____

_____

Is every rhombus a square?

_____

_____

2. Are all trapezoids also parallelograms?

trapezoid   parallelogram

_____

_____

3. Are all squares also parallelograms?

parallelogram   square

_____

_____

_____

4. Are all parallelograms also rectangles?

_____

_____

     Measuring Up® to the Georgia Performance Standards

CRCT Practice **Directions: Choose the best answer for each question.
Circle the letter for the answer you have chosen.**

1. Can any rectangles be parallelograms?

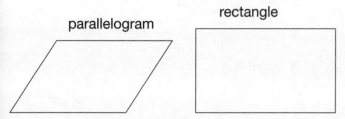

parallelogram   rectangle

A. No, because parallelograms only have one set of parallel lines.

B. No, because rectangles have two sets of parallel lines.

C. Yes, because they have two sets of parallel lines.

D. Yes, because all parallelograms have right angles.

2. Which feature do a square and a trapezoid have in common?

A. two sets of parallel lines

B. one set of parallel lines

C. congruent sides

D. right angles

 3. Keisha says that a rectangle can be a rhombus. Leon says a rectangle cannot be a rhombus. Which statement is true?

A. Leon is correct because a rectangle has 2 pairs of congruent sides.

B. Leon is correct because a rhombus can have parallel lines.

C. Keisha is correct because all rectangles are rhombuses.

D. Keisha is correct because some rectangles are squares and a square is a rhombus.

 4. Which statement is NOT true of the shapes shown below?

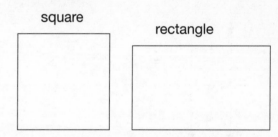

square   rectangle

A. Both are also parallelograms.

B. Both are also quadrilaterals.

C. Both have only two right angles.

D. Both have parallel and perpendicular sides.

Directions: Choose the best answer for each question.

Circle the letter for the answer you have chosen.

 1. Which of these shows two intersecting lines that are NOT perpendicular?

A.

B.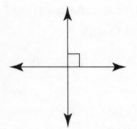

C.

D.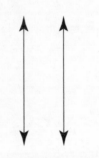

2. What kind of triangle is shown?

A. obtuse

B. right

C. acute

D. quadrilateral

3. Which describes where two faces of a rectangular prism meet?

A. side

B. vertex

C. point

D. edge

4. Which picture shows the half rotation of congruent figures?

A.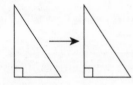

B.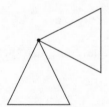

C.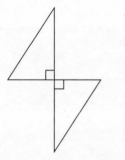

D.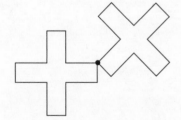

5. Which letters name two perpendicular line segments on the figure?

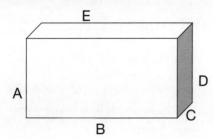

A. A and B

B. B and D

C. A and E

D. E and C

6. What is the ordered pair for the point that is 3 units to the right of point *B* and 2 units above point *B*?

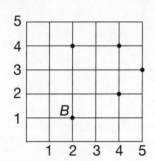

A. (4, 2)

B. (2, 4)

C. (5, 3)

D. (5, 2)

7. Which quadrilateral could NOT have two sets of parallel lines?

A. parallelogram

B. rectangle

C. square

D. trapezoid

8. Which figures are congruent?

A.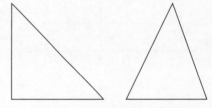

B.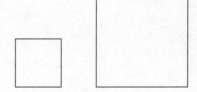

C.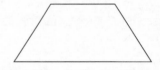

D.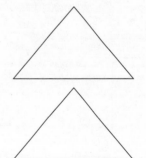

9. The coordinate grid shows a map of a neighborhood. Which ordered pair gives the location of the post office?

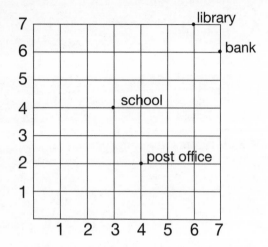

A. (7, 6)

B. (6, 7)

C. (2, 4)

D. (4, 2)

10. Which of these flat shapes could be used to make a cube?

A.

B.

C.

D.

11. Which statement is false?

A. A right triangle has one right angle.

B. A right triangle has one 90° angle.

C. An acute triangle has only one acute angle.

D. An obtuse triangle has only one obtuse angle.

12. Which is an accurate measurement of the angle?

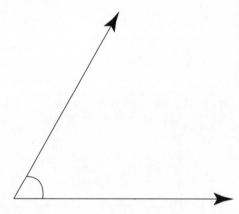

A. 50°

B. 55°

C. 60°

D. 65°

13. Alex takes two cubes of the same size and glues them together. If he lines up the edges of the cubes, what shape is he left with?

A. trapezoid

B. a rectangle

C. one rectangular prism

D. one large cube

14. Tonya needs to plot one more point on the grid to make a square. What is the ordered pair for the missing point?

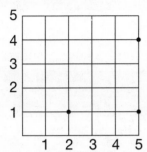

A. (4, 2)

B. (2, 4)

C. (2, 5)

D. (5, 2)

15. Which figure is similar to the figure shown below?

A.
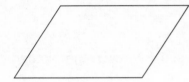

B.

C.

D.

16. Which is NOT true of both figures?

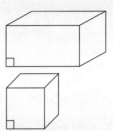

A. All sides of each figure are congruent.

B. They each have 6 faces.

C. They are rectangular prisms.

D. They each have 8 vertices.

17. How many lines of symmetry are in this figure?

A. 4

B. 2

C. 1

D. 0

18. Which description tells how these figures are related?

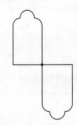

A. They are both prisms.

B. They have the same size and shape.

C. They show a full rotation.

D. They are both quadrilaterals.

M4D1.a	Represent data in bar, line, and pictographs.
M4D1.b	Investigate the features and tendencies of graphs.
M4P5	Student will create and use pictures, manipulatives, models, and symbols to organize, record, and communicate mathematical ideas.

You can use a pictograph to make information easier to see.

A **pictograph** is a graph that uses pictures or symbols and a key to show data.

A **key** tells what each picture or symbol stands for.

Guided Instruction

Problem

The table shows the votes of some fourth-grade students for their favorite type of TV shows. How does the pictograph show which is the students' favorite type of show?

Favorite Type of TV Show

Type of TV Show	Number of Votes
Comedy	60
Music	35
News	40
Drama	20

Title: _____

Type of TV Show	Number of Votes
Comedy	

Key: ▲ = _____ votes

Step 1 Write a title and the name of each type of TV show in the pictograph.

Step 2 Choose a number to use for the key. Since most of the data are multiples of 10, let each ▲ stands for ten votes. Complete the key.

Step 3 Draw the correct number of ▲ for each type of show to complete the graph. Use a half picture ◢ to show half the number given in the key.

Which type of TV show has the most ▲s next to it? _____

Solution

How does the pictograph show which is the students' favorite type of TV show? _____

_____

_____

Measuring Up® to the Georgia Performance Standards

Apply the GPS

Use the data in the table to make a pictograph below.

1. Write a title for the pictograph.

2. Write the types of sports in the left column of the pictograph.

3. Use the key. In the pictograph, draw the symbols for each type of book.

4. How can you check if the number of symbols in your graph is correct?

_____

_____

_____

5. Suppose each symbol means 6 votes. How many symbols would you draw for baseball? _____

Favorite Type of Sport

Type of Sport	Number of Votes
Skateboarding	6
Baseball	48
Hockey	30
Basketball	60

Title: _____

Type of Sport	Number of Votes

Key: ★ = _____ votes

Solve each problem.

6. In a pictograph, each ☐ stands for 50 meals sold at Barney's Hotel. The symbols below show the total number of meals sold.

☐ ☐ ☐ ☐

What is the total number of meals sold?

_____

7. How did you figure out the answer to number 6?

_____

_____

_____

8. Rosanna created a pictograph showing how many peaches each student picked. She used the symbol △ to stand for 20 peaches. Explain how Rosanna can show 90 peaches on the pictograph.

_____

_____

_____

CRCT Practice

Directions: Choose the best answer for each question. Circle the letter for the answer you have chosen.

1. Alex wants to make a pictograph to show the data in the table below. Which key should Alex use if he wants to have only whole symbols on his pictograph?

Favorite Color

Color	Number of Votes
Blue	35
Red	40
Yellow	20
Green	15

A. △ = 2 votes

B. △ = 5 votes

C. △ = 10 votes

D. △ = 35 votes

2. Jessie's class voted for their favorite pet. 16 of the students voted for a dog. If △ = 4 votes, which answer shows the vote for a dog on a pictograph?

A. △ △ △ △

B. △ △ △

C. △ △

D. △

3. The pictograph below shows the number of pets who live in each town.

Town	Pet Population
Ottisburg	◯◯◖
Eastown	◯◯◯◯◯
Greenville	◯◯◯◯◯◯◯◯
Oak City	◯◯◯◯◯◯◖

Key: ◯ = 5,000 pets

Which town has 40,000 pets?

A. Oak City

B. Eastown

C. Otisburg

D. Greenville

4. Chelsea's class made a pictograph to show how many books they read during vacation. The key is △ = 12 books. The pictograph showed ⟍ next to Chelsea's name. How many books did Chelsea read during the vacation?

A. 3

B. 6

C. 12

D. 24

Lesson 58 Interpret and Make Bar Graphs

M4D1.a Represent data in bar, line and pictographs.
M4D1.b Investigate the features and tendencies of graphs.
M4P5 Student will create and use pictures, manipulatives, models, and symbols to organize, record, and communicate mathematical ideas.

You can use a bar graph to compare and interpret a set of data. A **bar graph** uses bars of different lengths to show similar kinds of data. The bars can be vertical or horizontal. You can compare the lengths of the bars to find a trend or pattern in the data.

Guided Instruction

Problem

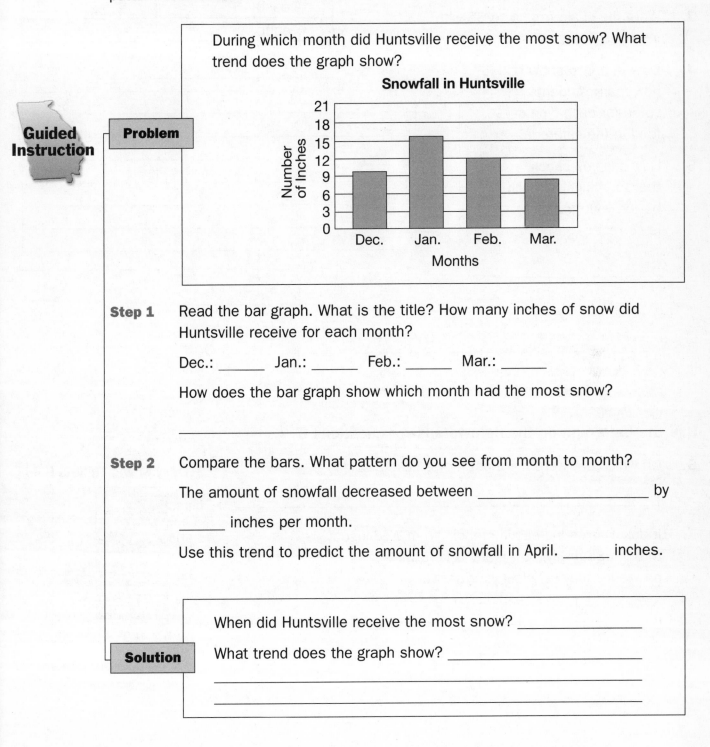

During which month did Huntsville receive the most snow? What trend does the graph show?

Snowfall in Huntsville

Step 1 Read the bar graph. What is the title? How many inches of snow did Huntsville receive for each month?

Dec.: _____ Jan.: _____ Feb.: _____ Mar.: _____

How does the bar graph show which month had the most snow?

_____

Step 2 Compare the bars. What pattern do you see from month to month?

The amount of snowfall decreased between _____ by

_____ inches per month.

Use this trend to predict the amount of snowfall in April. _____ inches.

Solution

When did Huntsville receive the most snow? _____

What trend does the graph show? _____

_____

_____

Apply the GPS

Use the data in the table to make a bar graph below.

1. Write a title for the bar graph.

2. Write labels at the side and bottom of the bar graph.

3. Write the scale from 0 to 35 with intervals of 5.

4. Draw a bar to show how many students voted for each type of food in the cafeteria.

5. How can you check that the height of each bar on your graph is correct?

Type of Cafeteria Food	Number of Votes
sandwiches	24
pizza	31
pasta	20
soup	16

Title: _____

_____

_____

_____

_____

Use the bar graph on the right to answer questions 6–7.

6. On which day were the most movie tickets sold?

_____

7. If ticket sales increased steadily from Wednesday through Saturday, how many tickets were sold on Wednesday? Explain your answer.

_____

_____

_____

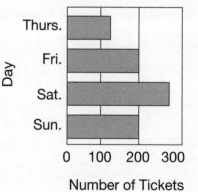

Daily Movie Tickets Sold

CRCT Practice

Directions: Choose the best answer for each question. Circle the letter for the answer you have chosen.

1. How many more oranges were sold than bananas?

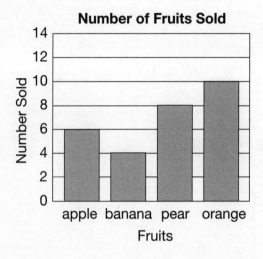

Number of Fruits Sold

A. 4

B. 6

C. 8

D. 10

2. Julie wants to make a bar graph of the number of boys and girls in her class. There are 20 students in her class. What intervals should she use to mark the side of her graph?

A. intervals of 2

B. intervals of 8

C. intervals of 10

D. intervals of 20

3. Which two types of dogs had the same number sold?

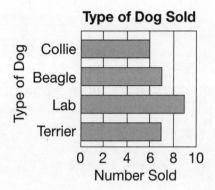

Type of Dog Sold

A. lab and collie

B. collie and beagle

C. terrier and beagle

D. terrier and lab

4. After taking his first test, Rob started studying with a tutor. What trend do Rob's test scores show?

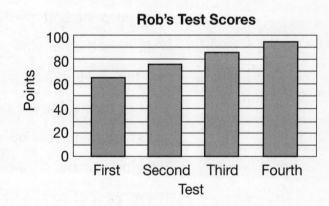

Rob's Test Scores

A. He scored the same on all 4 tests.

B. His scores went up and down.

C. His scores went down by 10 points on each test.

D. His scores improved by 10 points on each test.

Lesson 59 Interpret and Make Line Graphs

M4D1.a Represent data in bar, line, and pictographs.
M4D1.b Investigate the features and tendencies of graphs.

You can use a line graph to show data. A **line graph** shows how data change over a period of time. Each piece of data is shown with a point or dot on the graph. All of the points are then connected with a line. The **range** of a set of data is the difference between the greatest and least numbers, or the highest and lowest points on the line.

Guided Instruction

Problem Look at the line graph. What was the range of people waiting for tickets from 1:00 to 4:00?

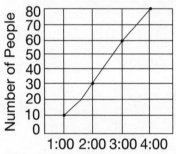

People Waiting for Tickets

Step 1 Look at the line graph carefully. What is the title of the graph?

_____

What does the bottom show? _____

What does the left side show? _____

Step 2 Find the range of people who waited in line for tickets each hour.

Start by finding the greatest and least numbers of people.

The greatest number of people is _____.

The least number of people is _____.

The number of people who waited for tickets ranged from _____ to _____ people.

Step 3 Subtract the least number of people from the greatest number of people to find the range. _____ − _____ = _____

Solution What is the range of people waiting for tickets? _____ people

Apply the GPS   **Use the data in the table to make a line graph.**

1. Write a title for the graph.

2. Label the sides of the graph. Write the number of the weeks on the bottom and the number of inches on the left side of the bar graph.

3. Put a point or dot on the graph for each number of weeks and number of inches. Then connect the dots with a line.

4. Between which two weeks did the seedling grow most? Explain how you know.

_____

_____

_____

_____

Height of Seedling

Week	Number of Inches
Week 1	0
Week 2	1
Week 3	3
Week 4	6

Title: _____

Use the line graph on the right to answer questions 5–7.

5. How many more cookies were sold in March than in January? _____

6. What is the range of cookies shown on the line graph? _____

7. Do you know how many cookies will be sold in April? Explain why or why not.

_____

_____

_____

_____

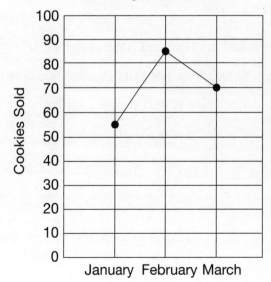

CRCT Practice

Directions: Choose the best answer for each question.
Circle the letter for the answer you have chosen.

1. Which information is NOT shown on the graph?

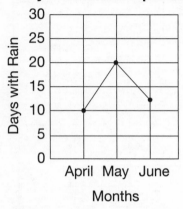

Days with Rainfall per Month

A. 10 days of rainfall in April

B. 20 days of rainfall in May

C. 15 days of rainfall in June

D. range of 10 days with rain

2. How can you find the range by reading a line graph?

A. Add the least and greatest numbers.

B. Subtract the least and greatest numbers.

C. The range is the greatest number.

D. The range is the least number.

3. What is the range of books sold during the three years shown on the line graph?

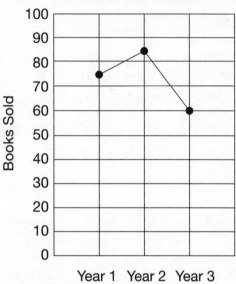

Books Sold in Three Years

A. 135

B. 75

C. 60

D. 25

4. Sasha wants to make a line graph to show how many inches her daisy has grown in one month. What should the title of Sasha's graph be?

A. 2 inches in Week 3

B. Daisy Week 1

C. Daisy Growth During 1 Month

D. Growth During 2 Weeks

Lesson 60 Interpret Data in Tables and Graphs

M4D1.d Identify missing information and duplications in data.
M4P5 Student will create and use pictures, manipulatives, models, and symbols to organize, record, and communicate mathematical ideas.

You can compare data in tables and graphs. You can tell how the data is alike and different. Sometimes information in a table is left out of a graph, or shown incorrectly. Some tables and graphs may also show duplicate information.

Guided Instruction

Problem Look at the table and the line graph below. What information is missing from the table that is included in the bar graph? What information is easier to see on the line graph?

Cars Washed

Day	Number of Cars
Friday	25
Saturday	39
Sunday	42
Monday	15

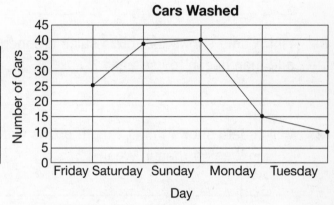

Step 1 Compare the table and graph. What do they both show?

_____

Step 2 What days of the week does the table show?

_____

What days of the week does the graph show?

_____

Step 3 Between which two days did the number of cars washed change the most? Compare the data from Friday through Monday

_____

Is it easier to compare changes in data using the table or the line graph?

_____

Solution What information is missing from the table? _____

_____ .

What is easier to see on the line graph? _____ .

Apply the GPS

Use the data in the table and graph to answer the questions below.

1. What information is duplicated or shown in both the table and graph?

_____

2. What information is shown in the table but missing from the line graph?

_____

3. Which data shows that pizza sales dropped and then began to rise again?

_____

4. Which data shows that 12 more pizzas were sold in Week 4 than in Week 1?

_____

Weekly Pizza Sales

Week	Number of Pizzas Sold
Week 1	15
Week 2	19
Week 3	31
Week 4	27

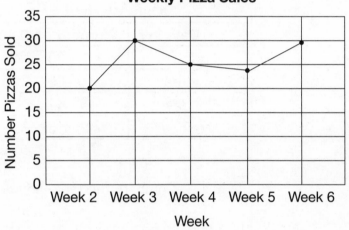

Weekly Pizza Sales

Use the table and graph to answer questions 5–8.

5. What information is given by both sets of data? _____

_____

6. Which set of data has more information?

_____

7. What is the extra information?

_____

_____

8. What should you look at first when comparing tables and graphs? Explain.

_____

_____

Tomato Plant Growth

Tomato Plant Growth

Month	Inches Grown
May	3
June	5
July	8
August	10

Directions: Choose the best answer for each question. Circle the letter for the answer you have chosen.

Use the graph and table to answer questions 1–2.

Art Supply Sales

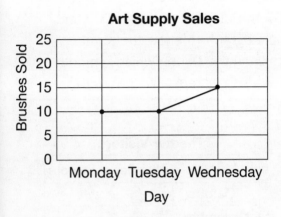

Art Supply Sales

Days	Brushes Sold
Tuesday	10
Wednesday	15
Thursday	20

1. What information that appears in the graph is missing from the table data?

   A. brushes sold on Monday

   B. brushes sold on Tuesday

   C. brushes sold on Wednesday

   D. brushes sold on Thursday

2. How many brushes were sold between Monday and Thursday?

   A. 10

   B. 45

   C. 55

   D. 65

Use the graph and table to answer questions 3–4.

Miles Jogged

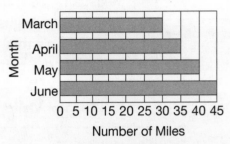

Miles Jogged

Month	Number of Miles
January	20
February	25
March	30
April	35

 3. Compare the data in the bar graph and table. Which of the following is NOT true?

   A. Both show 30 miles jogged in March.

   B. Both show 35 miles jogged in April.

   C. Only the table shows the miles jogged in January.

   D. Only the bar graph shows information for 4 months.

 4. What trend is shown by both the bar graph and the table?

   A. The miles jogged each month decreased by 10.

   B. The miles jogged each month increased by 5.

   C. More miles were jogged in the winter months.

   D. More miles were jogged in the spring months.

Lesson 61 Compare Graphs

M4D1.c Compare different graphical representations for a given set of data.

M4P4 Students will understand how mathematical ideas interconnect and build on one another and apply mathematics in other content areas.

You can compare the data on different types of graphs by identifying a trend. A **trend** is a pattern shown by the data. Trends often happen over a period of time.

Guided Instruction

Problem

Melissa made a bar graph to show the number of theater visitors from May to August. Bill made a pictograph to show the number of theater visitors from October to January. During which 4-month period did the number of theater visitors increase each month?

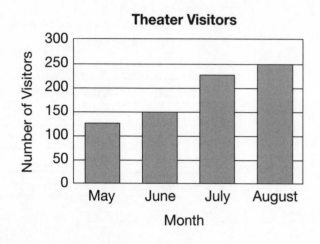

Theater Visitors

Month	Number of Visitors
October	🔶🔶🔶🔶
November	🔶🔶🔶
December	🔶🔶🔶
January	🔶🔶

Key 🔶 = 50 visitors

Step 1 List the data from the bar graph.

May: _____ visitors   July: _____ visitors

June: _____ visitors   August: _____ visitors

Step 2 List the data from the pictograph.

October: _____ visitors   December: _____ visitors

November: _____ visitors   January: _____ visitors

Step 3 Identify the trend in each group of data.

The bar graph shows an _____ in the number of visitors from month to month.

The pictograph shows a _____ in the number of visitors from month to month.

Solution

During which 4-month period did the number of theater visitors increase each month? _____

Measuring Up® to the Georgia Performance Standards

Apply the GPS

Use the graphs below to answer each question.

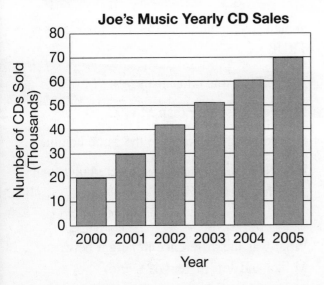

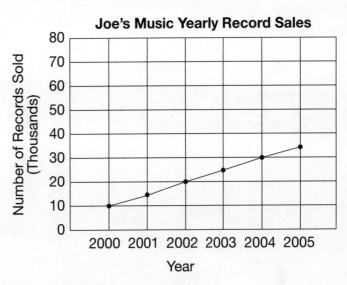

1. For which product, records or CDs, did the 2001 sales total 15,000?

_____

2. How many CDs were sold in 2000? How many records?

_____

3. Compare the number of records sold with the number of CDs sold in 2004. How many more CDs than records were sold that year? _____

4. What trend do you see in Joe's Music sales of CDs?

_____

Solve each problem. Use the graphs at the top of the page.

5. If the trend in record sales continues, how many records will be sold in 2006?

_____

6. If the trend in CD sales continues, how many CDs will be sold in 2006? Explain how you know. _____

_____

7. Explain how the two graphs are alike. _____

_____

_____

CRCT Practice

Directions: Choose the best answer for each question.
Circle the letter for the answer you have chosen.

 1. How are bar graphs and line graphs alike?

A. They always use the same scale.

B. Both show trends in data.

C. Both use points to show data.

D. Both use bars to show data.

Use the graphs below to answer questions 2–4.

Milika's Height

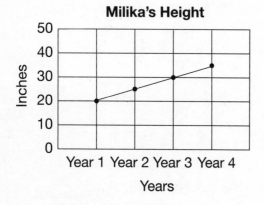

Jeff's Height

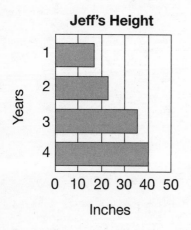

2. Which statement about the data for Year 3 is TRUE?

A. Milika was taller than Jeff.

B. Jeff was taller than Milika.

C. Jeff and Milika were the same height.

D. Neither Jeff nor Milika were taller than they were in Year 2.

3. What was the difference in height between Milika and Jeff in Year 4?

A. Jeff was 1 inch taller than Milika.

B. Milika was 1 inch taller than Jeff.

C. Jeff was 5 inches taller than Milika.

D. Milika was 5 inches taller than Jeff.

 4. How are the trends of the two graphs shown differently?

A. The trend on the line graph is read from top to bottom.

B. The trend on the bar graph is read from left to right.

C. The trend on the bar graph is shown with a trend line.

D. The trend on the line graph is read from left to right.

     Measuring Up® to the Georgia Performance Standards

Focus on GPS

Lesson 62 **Problem-Solving Strategy: Make an Organized List**

M4P1.b   Solve single and multi-step routine word problems related to all appropriate fourth-grade math standards.

You can make an organized list to help solve problems. Write out all of the possible outcomes to find out how many ways you can solve a problem.

Guided Instruction

Problem	Jackie needs to buy a $0.37 stamp. The stamp vending machine accepts only dimes and pennies. How many different coin combinations could Jackie use to pay for the stamp?

Understand the problem.

What do you need to find out?

_____

_____

List what you know.

What is the cost of the stamp? _____

What coins can you use? _____

Make a plan.

You can make a list to solve this problem.

Pennies	Value	Dimes	Value	Total
37	$0.37	0	$0.00	$0.37
_____	$0.27	1	$0.10	$0.37
17	$0.17	2	$0.20	$0.37
7	$0.07	_____	$0.30	$0.37

Solve the problem.

How many different coin combinations could Jackie use to pay for the stamp? _____

Check your answer.

Make sure your list is complete. Check that you have used every possible combination of dimes and pennies to make $0.37.

Apply the GPS

Solve each problem by making a list.

Work Space

1. Suppose you have $0.80 in quarters and nickels. How many different combinations of coins could you have? What are they?

_____

_____

_____

2. A group of people spent $15.00 for play tickets. If adult tickets cost $3.00 and children's tickets cost $1.00, how many possible combinations of children and adults could have bought tickets? What are they? _____

_____

_____

3. Margo had a picture of her cat, dog, and hamster in her wallet. One picture is in the front, one is in the middle, and one is in the back. How many different ways can Margo put the pictures in her wallet?

_____

4. Oscar has only dimes and nickels in his pocket. The value of the coins totals $0.50. List the possible coins that he could have.

_____

_____

_____

CRCT Practice

Directions: Choose the best answer for each question.
Circle the letter for the answer you have chosen.

1. The total value of 3 coins is $0.60. The coins are quarters and dimes. How many of each coin are there?

   A. 2 dimes, 1 quarter

   B. 3 quarters, 0 dimes

   C. 2 quarters, 1 dime

   D. 0 quarters, 3 dimes

2. Joseph wants to arrange his garden into three rows: carrots, tomatoes, and cucumbers. In how many ways could he arrange the garden?

   A. 10 ways

   B. 9 ways

   C. 8 ways

   D. 6 ways

3. Hal has 4 quarters and 10 dimes. How many different ways can he make $1.00?

   A. 2 ways

   B. 3 ways

   C. 6 ways

   D. 8 ways

4. Wendy wants to rearrange the clothes in her dresser. Her dresser has three drawers. She puts socks, shirts, and jeans in her dresser. How many different ways can she arrange her clothing?

   A. 2 ways

   B. 3 ways

   C. 6 ways

   D. 8 ways

5. Jacob can do his homework in any order he wants. He has to do math, social studies, and science homework. He does not want to do his math homework first. How many ways can he do his homework?

   A. 2 ways

   B. 4 ways

   C. 6 ways

   D. 8 ways

**Directions: Choose the best answer for each question.
Circle the letter for the answer you have chosen.**

1. How many cheese snacks were sold?

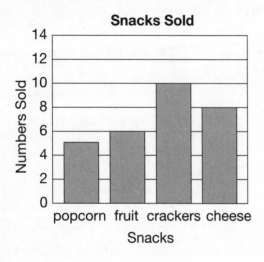

Snacks Sold

A. 5

B. 6

C. 8

D. 10

2. Mr. Lee can grade his students' papers in any order he wants. He has to grade essays, tests, and pop quizzes. He does not want to grade the pop quizzes first. How many ways can he grade the papers?

A. 8 ways

B. 6 ways

C. 4 ways

D. 2 ways

3. What kind of graph makes it easy to see changes in data over a period of time?

A. bar graph

B. line graph

C. pictograph

D. circle graph

4. What information that appears in the graph is missing from the table data?

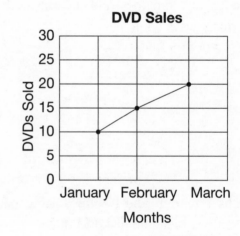

DVD Sales

Months	DVDs Sold
February	15
March	20
April	25

A. DVDs sold in January

B. DVDs sold in February

C. DVDs sold in March

D. DVDs sold in April

5. Which two fruits had the same number of containers sold?

Types of Fruit Sold

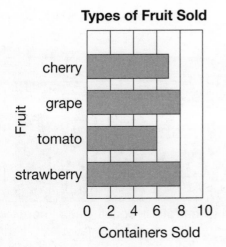

A. strawberry and tomato

B. cherry and grape

C. cherry and strawberry

D. grape and strawberry

6. Sarah's soccer team voted on what they wanted for lunch. 9 of the players voted for sandwiches. If △ = 2 votes, which answer shows the vote for a sandwiches on a pictograph?

A. △ ⟍

B. △ △

C. △ △ △ ⟍

D. △ △ △ △ ⟍

7. During which week were both plants the same size?

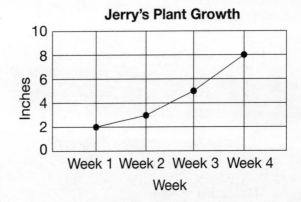

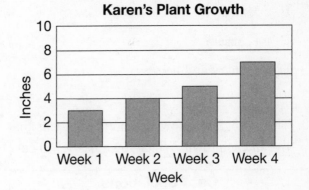

A. Week 1

B. Week 2

C. Week 3

D. Week 4

8. Terence wants to arrange his toys into three rows: soldiers, jacks, and cars. In how many ways could he arrange the toys?

A. 6 ways

B. 8 ways

C. 9 ways

D. 10 ways

9. Which month had about 10 days of snowfall?

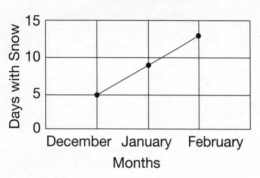

Days with Snow

A. December

B. January

C. February

D. January and February

10. The pictograph shows the number of cats that live in each town. Which town has 1,500 cats?

Cat Populations	
Town	**Cat Population**
Lewisville	O)
East Carlsburg	O O O
Pine Woods	O O O O O
Hamptonville	O O O O)

Key: O = 1,000 cats

A. Lewisville

B. East Carlsburg

C. Pine Woods

D. Hamptonville

11. How many more packages of peas were sold than broccoli?

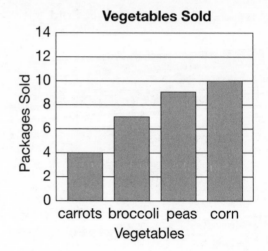

Vegetables Sold

A. 2

B. 7

C. 9

D. 10

12. Jack has 2 dimes and 8 nickels. How many different ways can he make $0.50?

A. 2 ways

B. 3 ways

C. 6 ways

D. 8 ways

13. What is the range of beach balls sold during the three days shown on the bar graph?

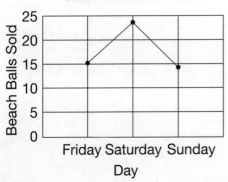

Sales of Beach Balls

A. 40

B. 25

C. 15

D. 10

14. The total value of a stack of quarters and dimes is $0.65. How many of each coin are there?

A. 2 quarters, 1 dime

B. 2 quarters, 3 dimes

C. 1 quarter, 4 dimes

D. 1 quarter, 3 dimes

15. Juanita wants to make a bar graph of the number of cats and dogs at Spike's Pet Shop. There are 12 pets in the shop. What intervals should she use to mark the side of her graph?

A. intervals of 2

B. intervals of 8

C. intervals of 10

D. intervals of 12

16. Mrs. Ryan wants to make a bar graph to show how many pints of each kind of ice cream she sold this week. She sold three different kinds of ice cream. What would the title of Mrs. Ryan's graph be?

A. Grocery Store

B. Chocolate, Vanilla, Strawberry

C. Ice Cream Sales This Week

D. Ice Cream Sales Today

17. Larry is making a line graph to show how many hours he spent on homework for each week. The most hours he spent in one week was 12. He kept track of his hours for 8 weeks. Which of the following is true?

A. The graph will have 12 plotted points.

B. The highest point on the trend line will be 12 hours.

C. The scale of hours will go from 0 to 8.

D. You will not be able to tell the range of the data from the graph.

End-of-Book
Applying Concepts

The end-of-book **Applying Concepts** is a

comprehensive review of all the

Georgia Mathematics Performance Standards

covered in the lessons.

By practicing with these challenging,

broad-based, higher-level thinking questions,

you will be building up your stamina

to succeed on the CRCT

and in other academic endeavors

that require higher-level thinking.

Directions: Choose the best answer for each question.
Circle the letter for the answer you have chosen.

1. What decimal matches the model?

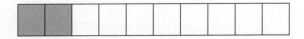

   A. 20.0

   B.   2.0

   C.   0.2

   D.   0.02

2. Which number shows this amount rounded to the nearest whole dollar?

   A. $2.00

   B. $2.20

   C. $2.23

   D. $3.00

3. Which list does NOT show the numbers ordered from greatest to least?

   A. 82.15, 81.98, 81.97

   B. 23.29, 20.48, 20.12

   C. 53.91, 53.85, 53.86

   D. 22.94, 22.23, 22.12

4. Find the quotient.

$$50\overline{)2{,}550}$$

   A. 25

   B. 50

   C. 51

   D. 250

5. Which has the same answer as $9{,}090 \div 30$?

   A. $90 - 30$

   B. $909 \div 15$

   C. $909 \div 3$

   D. $9090 \div 3$

6. Using front-end estimation, estimate the total number of viewers in all three theaters listed below.

Movie Viewers

Theater	Number of Viewers
Theater 1	302
Theater 2	154
Theater 3	214

A. 400

B. 500

C. 600

D. 700

7. Which is an example of an obtuse triangle?

A.

B.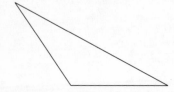

C.

D.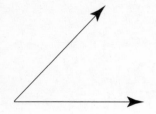

8. Monica has a rectangular prism. If she cuts the long side of the prism in half, which two solid figures will she have?

A. one cube and one rectangular prism

B. two cubes

C. two rectangular prisms

D. one rectangular prism and one triangular prism

9. What is the value of the underlined digit in 7,301?

A.   7

B.   70

C.   700

D.   7,000

10. Find the sum.

$$0.34 + 0.10 + 0.55 =$$

A. 0.99

B. 0.88

C. 0.85

D. 0.73

11. Which number sentence does this array represent?

$$\triangle \triangle \triangle \triangle \triangle \triangle$$
$$\triangle \triangle \triangle \triangle \triangle \triangle$$
$$\triangle \triangle \triangle \triangle \triangle \triangle$$
$$\triangle \triangle \triangle \triangle \triangle \triangle$$

A. $4 + 4 + 4 + 4 = 16$

B. $4 + 6 = 10$

C. $4 \times 6 = 24$

D. $6 \times 6 = 36$

12. About how long is the rectangle?

├──────┤
2 units

A. 4 units

B. 6 units

C. 8 units

D. 10 units

13. What is the missing divisor?

$$221 \div \boxed{} = 13$$

A. 12

B. 17

C. 157

D. 208

14. Danielle is seating customers in her restaurant. There are 6 tables, with 2 customers waiting for each table. What is the best way to figure out how many customers are waiting?

A. estimate

B. paper and pencil

C. mentally

D. calculator

15. If George started shopping at 12:25 and he finished at 4:40, how long did it take George to do his shopping?

A. 4 hours and 10 minutes

B. 4 hours and 15 minutes

C. 4 hours and 25 minutes

D. 5 hours and 25 minutes

16. The table shows the height of four different towers.

Height of Buildings

Name	Height in Feet
Mom's Tower	1,380
Pop's Tower	1,649
Babe's Tower	921
Junior's Tower	989

Which is the height of Pop's Tower rounded to the nearest hundred?

A. 1,400 feet

B. 1,600 feet

C. 1,650 feet

D. 1,700 feet

17. There were 667 shoppers at Food Fest on Saturday. There were 582 shoppers on Sunday. Using rounding, what is an estimate of the total number of people who shopped there both days?

A. 1,100

B. 1,200

C. 1,300

D. 1,400

18. The number 500,000 + 7,000 + 100 + 50 + 0 is written in expanded form. Which is the number in word form?

A. five hundred thousand, seventy-one hundred five

B. five thousand, seven hundred, fifteen

C. five hundred seven thousand, one hundred fifty

D. fifty-seven thousand, one hundred fifty

19. What fraction names the shaded part?

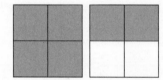

A. $\frac{1}{4}$

B. $\frac{2}{8}$

C. $1\frac{1}{2}$

D. $1\frac{2}{3}$

20. Dorell's class voted on their favorite kind of book. Six of the students voted for mystery books. If $\varnothing$ = 3 votes, which answer shows the votes for mystery books on a pictograph?

A. $\varnothing$

B. $\varnothing\varnothing$

C. $\varnothing\varnothing\varnothing$

D. $\varnothing\varnothing\varnothing\varnothing\varnothing\varnothing$

21. The table below shows the total number of pages in different magazines.

Pages in Magazine

Magazine Title	Number of Pages
Sports This Week	259
Sports This Month	823
Style and Beauty	615
News for All	405

Which two magazines have the greatest difference in number of pages?

A. Sports This Month and News for All

B. Sports This Month and Sports This Week

C. Style and Beauty and Sports This Week

D. News for All and Style and Beauty

22. Which fraction is NOT equivalent to the fraction shown in the model?

A. $\frac{2}{4}$

B. $\frac{4}{8}$

C. $\frac{1}{2}$

D. $\frac{1}{4}$

23. The graph below shows the sales of four items used in sports.

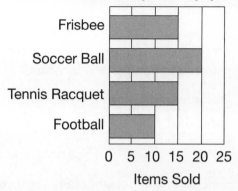

Which two items sold equally well?

A. tennis racquet and football

B. Frisbee and soccer ball

C. Frisbee and tennis racquet

D. football and soccer ball

24. Which fraction represents the area that is NOT shaded?

A. $\frac{1}{10}$

B. $\frac{1}{5}$

C. $\frac{4}{5}$

D. $\frac{7}{10}$

25. Mr. Chang wants to make a double line graph to show how many more cars were sold this month than last month. What would the title of Mr. Chang's graph be?

   A.   Mr. Chang's Sales

   B.   Car Sale Comparison by Month

   C.   Car Sales This Month

   D.   Car Sales Last Month

26. Jack helped paint a doghouse red and yellow. The shaded parts in the model show the amounts of paint left in the jars. How many more jars of red paint did they use than jars of yellow paint?

   Red Paint   Yellow Paint

   A. $\frac{2}{8}$ jar

   B. $\frac{3}{8}$ jar

   C. $\frac{1}{2}$ jar

   D. $\frac{3}{4}$ jar

27. What is the missing factor?

$$11 \times \boxed{} = 154$$

   A.   12

   B.   13

   C.   14

   D.   131

28. Use a rule to find the numbers that are missing.

In	81		18
Out	9		2

   A.   36, 8

   B.   45, 9

   C.   54, 6

   D.   82, 7

29. Find the product.

$$(7 \times 2) \times 9 =$$

   A.   23

   B.   90

   C.   126

   D.   132

30. Which numbers are in order from least to greatest?

   A.   0.60, 0.63, 0.41, 0.07

   B.   0.25, 0.29, 0.55, 0.87

   C.   0.06, 0.09, 0.45, 0.44

   D.   0.28, 0.66, 0.32, 0.45

31. At the store, Gus bought some bread, eggs, and milk. The total cost was $7.39. He paid the cashier $8.00. How many pennies must he get back?

    A. one

    B. four

    C. eight

    D. nine

32. Which equation matches the model?

    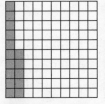 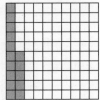

    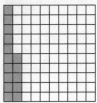

    A. $2 \times 0.15 = 0.30$

    B. $3 \times 0.15 = 0.45$

    C. $3 + 0.15 = 3.15$

    D. $2 \times 0.30 = 0.6$

33. Mrs. Lee buys 5 boxes of cookies from children in her neighborhood. She buys three boxes for $2.00 each. She buys two boxes for $2.50 each. How much money does Mrs. Lee spend on the cookies in all?

    A. $7.00

    B. $8.00

    C. $11.00

    D. $15.00

34. Which of these shows perpendicular intersecting lines?

    A.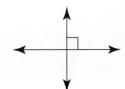

    B.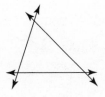

    C.

    D.

35. What is the ordered pair for the point that is 2 units to the right of point A and 3 units above point A?

    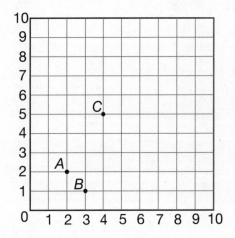

    A. (4, 5)

    B. (6, 8)

    C. (4, 4)

    D. (6, 5)

36. Which fraction is equal to the sum of the shaded models?

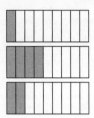

   A. $\frac{2}{3}$

   B. $\frac{1}{3}$

   C. $\frac{6}{9}$

   D. $\frac{7}{9}$

37. Which fraction is equal to the one below?

   A. $\frac{2}{5}$

   B. $\frac{4}{5}$

   C. $\frac{3}{10}$

   D. $\frac{1}{6}$

38. Use the model to divide 0.6 by 3.

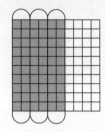

   A. 20

   B. 2

   C. 0.2

   D. 0.02

39. Greg is going to walk 8.7 miles on Saturday. He will stop three times during the walk. All four sections of the walk will be equal. How far will Greg walk during each section of his walk?

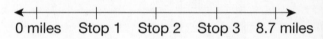

0 miles   Stop 1   Stop 2   Stop 3   8.7 miles

   A. 1.74 miles

   B. 2.3 miles

   C. 2.175 miles

   D. 2.9 miles

40. Which statement is true?

    A. A hexagon has five sides.

    B. A right triangle has two right angles.

    C. An acute triangle has two perpendicular lines.

    D. A right triangle has one 90° angle.

41. Which is the true statement about this figure?

    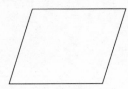

    A. It has four right angles.

    B. It has four obtuse angles.

    C. It has no lines of symmetry.

    D. It has one line of symmetry.

42. Which operations make the following equation true?

    $$(5 \boxed{} 8) + (2 \boxed{} 3) = 19$$

    A. ×, +

    B. +, ×

    C. +, +

    D. ×, ×

43. What is the total number of crayon boxes a large crate can hold?

    School Supply Store

Size of Crate	Number of Cartons	Number of Crayon Boxes in Each Carton
Large	24	14
Small	12	21

    A. 418

    B. 336

    C. 252

    D. 193

44. Which number sentence does this array represent?

    ▲ ▲ ▲ ▲ ▲ ▲
    ▲ ▲ ▲ ▲ ▲ ▲
    ▲ ▲ ▲ ▲ ▲ ▲
    ▲ ▲ ▲ ▲ ▲ ▲
    ▲ ▲ ▲ ▲ ▲ ▲

    A. 6 × 6 = 36

    B. 5 × 6 = 30

    C. 5 + 6 = 11

    D. 5 + 5 + 5 + 5 + 5 = 25

45. How many pepperoni pizzas were sold?

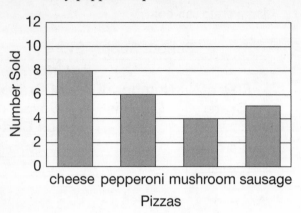

A.   4

B.   5

C.   6

D.   8

46. Which is true of both figures?

A.   There are no congruent faces on
either figure.

B.   They have the same number of vertices.

C.   They have the same number of faces.

D.   They are both prisms.

47. The perimeter of this figure is 54 feet. What
is the length of the missing side?

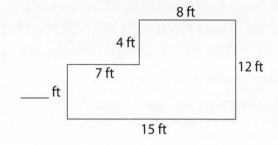

A.   6 feet

B.   7 feet

C.   8 feet

D.   9 feet

48. Which is an accurate measurement of
the angle?

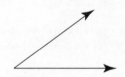

A.   30°

B.   40°

C.   50°

D.   60°

49. Which unit would be used to measure the length of a car?

    A. ton

    B. meter

    C. gram

    D. kilometer

50. Wilhelm has four coins in his pocket. The total value of the coins is $0.70. What combination of coins does Wilhelm have?

    A. 2 quarters and 2 dimes

    B. 3 quarters and 1 nickel

    C. 1 quarter, 2 dimes, and 1 nickel

    D. 2 quarters and 2 nickels

51. Ben put a deck of cards on a scale to find its weight. Which of these could be the weight of the cards?

    A. 10 inches

    B. 10 pounds

    C. 10 grams

    D. 10 kilograms

52. What operation would make all of the number sentences true?

    $$25 \boxed{} 5 = 5$$
    $$36 \boxed{} 9 = 4$$
    $$72 \boxed{} 8 = 9$$

    A. $+$

    B. $-$

    C. $\times$

    D. $\div$

53. Abby is reading a novel. Each day, she reads 15 more pages than the day before. If she read 98 pages on Tuesday, how many pages will she read on Friday?

    A. 158 pages

    B. 143 pages

    C. 128 pages

    D. 113 pages

54. The two graphs below show how much Olivia and Kim grew each month.

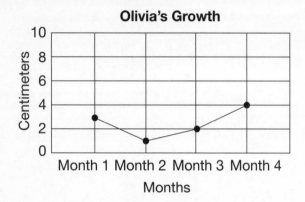

Olivia's Growth

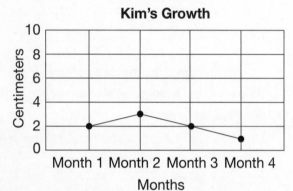

Kim's Growth

During which two months did Olivia grow more than Kim?

A. Months 1 and 2

B. Months 2 and 3

C. Months 3 and 4

D. Months 1 and 4

55. Which symbol belongs in the box to make a true number sentence?

$(10 \times 5) + 4$ ☐ $3 \times (15 + 3)$

A. =

B. ↑

C. <

D. >

56. Ben is collecting toy cars and trucks. He has 9 more toy cars than trucks. Let t stand for the number of trucks in his collection. How many toy cars does he have?

A. $t + 9$

B. $9 - t$

C. $t \times 9$

D. $9 \div t$

57. What rule can you apply to each "In" number to get each "Out" number?

In	Out
8	16
12	20
15	23

A. Multiply by 2.

B. Multiply by 2 and add 1.

C. Add 8.

D. Add 10.

58. Read the temperature for Sunday morning. The temperature on Sunday afternoon was 9° warmer than it was in the morning. What was the temperature on Sunday afternoon?

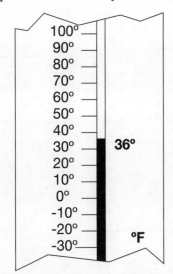

Sunday Morning Temperature

A. 46°F

B. 45°F

C. 36°F

D. 27°F

59. About how much does a basketball weigh?

A. 20 grams

B. 20 kilograms

C. 20 pounds

D. 20 ounces

60. Use both the graph and table below.

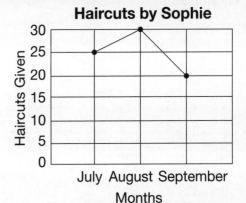

Haircuts by Sophie

Months	Haircuts Given
August	30
September	20
October	25

What information that appears in the graph is missing from the table data?

A. Haircuts given in July

B. Haircuts given in August

C. Haircuts given in September

D. Haircuts given in October

61. What number is missing from the table?

n	× 6
7	42
4	24
	54

A. 36

B. 30

C. 9

D. 6

62. Which letters name two parallel line segments on the figure?

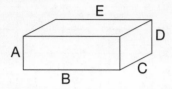

A. C and D

B. B and A

C. E and B

D. E and C

63. The coordinate grid shows a map of a classroom. Which ordered pair gives the location of the science center?

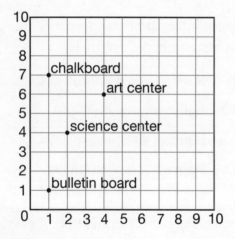

A. (1, 7)

B. (4, 6)

C. (2, 4)

D. (1, 1)

64. Which of these shapes can be made from 6 squares?

A.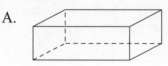

B.

C.

D.

65. Anthony is baking several recipes today. Three recipes each call for 2 eggs. One recipe calls for 4 eggs. Two other recipes call for 1 egg each. Which expression shows how many eggs Anthony needs altogether?

A. $(3 + 2) \times 4 + 2$

B. $3 + 2 + 4 + 2$

C. $(3 \times 2) + 4 + (2 \times 2)$

D. $(3 \times 2) + 4 + 2$

66. Which picture shows the half rotation of congruent figures?

A.

B.

C.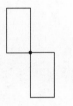

D.

67. Which number is a multiple of 7?

A. 32

B. 36

C. 42

D. 58

68. Find the product:

$$15 \times 23 =$$

A. 38

B. 251

C. 345

D. 468

69. Which figures are congruent?

A.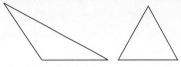

B.

C.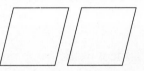

D.

70. Rachel can make a bouquet of any flowers in her garden. She has daisies, tulips, and roses in the garden. How many ways can she make a bouquet?

A. 8 ways

B. 7 ways

C. 6 ways

D. 4 ways

71. The school owns 4 school buses. Each bus can hold 55 students. How many students can ride on all the buses at once?

   A.   59

   B.   200

   C.   220

   D.   275

72. Jessica ran 3,249 feet in the competition. What is the expanded form of the number 3,249?

   A.   3,000 + 200 + 4 + 9

   B.   3,000 + 200 + 40 + 9

   C.   30,000 + 200 + 49

   D.   30,000 + 20 + 9

73. Charlie wants to paint a flag with three horizontal stripes: blue, black, and yellow. In how many ways could he order the stripes on the flag?

   A.   3 ways

   B.   4 ways

   C.   6 ways

   D.   8 ways

74. Jonah's running time in a race was 72.05 seconds. Sarah's running time in the same race was 3.7 seconds faster. Which of the following was Sarah's running time in the race?

   A.   68.25 seconds

   B.   68.35 seconds

   C.   75.75 seconds

   D.   76.62 seconds

75. Which quadrilateral has only right angles?

   A.   parallelogram

   B.   rectangle

   C.   rhombus

   D.   trapezoid

76. Jake's Tree Service is selling new trees. He has 12 rows of seedling trees. Each row will have 4 evergreen trees and 8 fruit trees. How many trees will Jake be selling in all?

   A.   24

   B.   114

   C.   144

   D.   156

Glossary

A

acute angle an angle measuring less than 90° (Lesson 51)

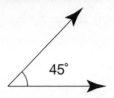

acute triangle a triangle having three acute angles (Lesson 51)

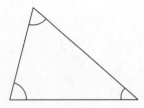

addition putting parts together (Lesson 22)

angle formed when two rays share an endpoint (Lesson 50)

area model a rectangular grid formed from unit squares (Lesson 13)

array a set of items arranged in rows and columns (Lesson 12)

Associative Property the way factors are grouped does not change the product (Lesson 11)

Example: (4 × 6) × 3 = 4 × (6 × 3)

B

bar graph a graph using bars of different lengths to show similar kinds of data (Lesson 58)

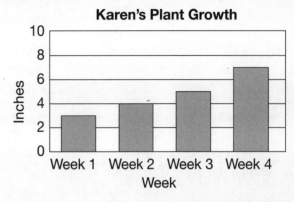

C

centimeter (cm) a metric unit of length that is used to measure small objects (Lesson 44)

Commutative Property changing the order of the factors does not change the product (Lesson 11)

Example: 2 × 4 = 4 × 2

compatible numbers numbers that are close to the actual numbers and that divide easily (Lesson 21)

composite number a whole number that has more than two factors (Lesson 10)

congruent figures that have the same shape and size (Lesson 54)

cube a type of rectangular prism made up of 6 square faces that are the same size (Lesson 53)

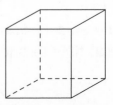

D

decimal a number that has one or more digits to the right of a decimal point, such as 1.75 or 0.8 (Lesson 30)

decimeter (dm) a metric unit of length that is equal to 10 centimeters (Lesson 44)

degrees measurement of the size of an angle (Lesson 50)

degrees Fahrenheit (°F) customary unit for temperature (Lesson 48)

denominator the bottom part of a fraction, which shows the total number of equal parts in the whole or group (Lesson 23)

Distributive Property to multiply a sum by a number, you can multiply each addend by the number and then add the products (Lesson 11)

Example: 4 × (5 + 2) = (4 × 5) + (4 × 2)

dividend the number being divided (Lesson 17)

division separating a whole into equal parts (Lesson 22)

divisor the number you are dividing by (Lesson 17)

E

edge a line segment where two faces meet (Lesson 53)

elapsed time the amount of time that passes from one time to another (Lesson 48)

equivalent fractions two or more fractions that have the same value (Lesson 24)

estimate a number close to an exact number (Lesson 4)

expression uses numbers, operations, and symbols or letters called variables to describe a word problem (Lesson 42)

F

faces the sides of a 3-dimensional figure (Lesson 53)

fact family a group of related addition and subtraction or multiplication and division facts that use the same set of whole numbers (Lesson 16)

factor a number that is multiplied to get a product (Lesson 9)

foot (ft) a standard unit of length that is equal to 12 inches (Lesson 44)

fraction a part of a whole or part of a group (Lesson 23)

full rotation moves a figure around a point back to its starting position (Lesson 54)

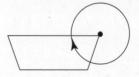

G

gram (g) a metric unit of mass that is approximately equal to the mass of a large paper clip (Lesson 46)

     Measuring Up® to the Georgia Performance Standards

I

improper fraction a fraction that shows an amount equal to or greater than 1 (Lesson 23)

inch (in.) a standard unit of length that is used to measure small objects (Lesson 44)

intersecting lines lines that meet or intersect at one point (Lesson 49)

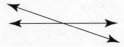

K

key tells what each picture or symbol on a pictograph stands for (Lesson 57)

kilogram (kg) a metric unit of mass that is equal to 1,000 grams (Lesson 46)

kilometer (km) a metric unit of length that is equal to 1,000 meters (Lesson 44)

L

line a straight path that extends in two directions (Lesson 49)

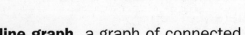

line graph a graph of connected points showing how data changes over a period of time (Lesson 59)

line of symmetry the line around which a figure is folded to make two congruent parts (Lesson 54)

line segment part of a line with two endpoints (Lesson 49)

M

mass how much matter something has (Lesson 46)

meter (m) a metric unit of length that is equal to 100 centimeters (Lesson 44)

mile (mi) a standard unit of length that is equal to 5,280 feet (Lesson 44)

millimeter (mm) a metric unit of length that is equal to one tenth of a centimeter (Lesson 44)

mixed number a number that is made up of a whole number and a fraction and shows an amount greater than 1 (Lesson 23)

multiple the product of a number and any other whole number (Lesson 9)

multiplication an operation in which equal groups are combined (Lessons 9, 22)

N

numerator the top part of a fraction, which shows how many parts you are counting (Lesson 23)

O

obtuse angle an angle measuring more than 90° (Lesson 51)

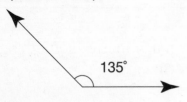

obtuse triangle a triangle with one obtuse angle (Lesson 51)

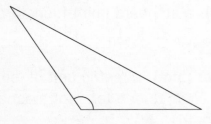

ordered pair a pair of numbers that gives the location of a point (Lesson 55)

ounce (oz) a standard unit of weight that is approximately equal to the weight of a small battery (Lesson 45)

P

parallel lines lines that never intersect and are the same distance apart everywhere (Lesson 49)

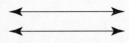

parallelogram a quadrilateral with opposite sides that are parallel and equal in length (Lesson 52)

perimeter the total distance around a figure (Lesson 47)

perpendicular lines lines that intersect and form square corners (Lesson 49)

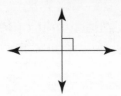

pictograph a graph that uses pictures or symbols and a key to show data (Lesson 57)

Town	Pet Population
Ottisburg	◯◯◖
Eastown	◯◯◯◯◯
Greenville	◯◯◯◯◯◯◯◯
Oak City	◯◯◯◯◯◯◖

Key: ◯ = 5,000 pets

pound (lb) a standard unit of weight that is equal to 16 ounces (Lesson 45)

prime number a whole number whose only factors are 1 and itself (Lesson 10)

prism a 3-dimensional or solid figure (Lesson 53)

product the result of multiplying two or more numbers (Lesson 9)

proper fraction a fraction that shows an amount less than 1 (Lesson 23)

protractor device used to measure and draw angles (Lesson 50)

Q

quadrilateral a closed shape made from four line segments, or sides (Lesson 52)

 Measuring Up® to the Georgia Performance Standards

quotient the answer in a division problem (Lesson 17)

R

range the difference between the greatest and least numbers, or the highest and lowest points on a line graph (Lesson 59)

ray a part of a line with one endpoint (Lesson 50)

rectangle a quadrilateral consisting of 4 right angles with opposite sides parallel and equal in length (Lesson 52)

rectangular prism a 3-dimensional figure made up of six sides, or faces, that are all rectangles (Lesson 53)

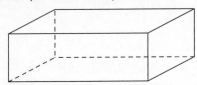

regroup to rename a number (Lesson 6)

related facts multiplication and division facts that are in the same fact family (Lesson 16)

remainder the amount left over when a number cannot be evenly divided (Lesson 18)

rhombus a quadrilateral having opposite sides that are parallel and all 4 sides equal in length (Lesson 52)

right angle an angle measuring exactly 90° (Lesson 51)

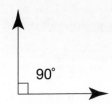

right triangle a triangle with one right angle (Lesson 51)

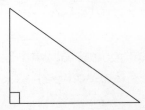

rotation moves a figure around a point (Lesson 54)

round a way to adjust numbers to the nearest ten, hundred, and so on in order to estimate an answer (Lesson 4)

rule tells you how the numbers in a pattern change, or how they are related (Lesson 39)

S

sides a group of three or more line segments that form a figure (Lesson 52)

similar figures that have the same shape but can be different sizes (Lesson 54)

square a quadrilateral with 4 right angles, opposite sides that are parallel, and all 4 sides equal in length (Lesson 52)

subtraction separating a part from a whole (Lesson 22)

symmetry the quality possessed by figures that can be folded on a line to make two congruent parts (Lesson 54)

T

temperature how hot or cold something is (Lesson 48)

ton a standard unit of weight that is equal to 2,000 pounds (Lesson 45)

trapezoid a quadrilateral with 1 pair of parallel sides (Lesson 52)

trend a pattern shown by the data on a graph that happens over a period of time (Lesson 61)

V

variables symbols or letters that stand for unknown amounts (Lesson 42)

vertex the shared endpoint of an angle or of three or more edges (Lessons 50, 53)

W

weight how heavy something is (Lesson 45)

Y

yard (yd) a standard unit of length that is equal to 3 feet (Lesson 44)

Measuring Up® to the Georgia Performance Standards